THE CONVERSATION OF HUMANITY

Page-Barbour Lectures
for 2005

The Conversation
of Humanity

⸺ഝഝ⸺

STEPHEN MULHALL

UNIVERSITY OF VIRGINIA PRESS
CHARLOTTESVILLE AND LONDON

University of Virginia Press
© 2007 by the Rector and Visitors of the
University of Virginia
All rights reserved

First published 2007

1 3 5 7 9 8 6 4 2

LIBRARY OF CONGRESS CATALOGING-IN-PUBLICATION DATA
Mulhall, Stephen, 1962–
The conversation of humanity / Stephen Mulhall.
p.   cm. — (Page-Barbour lectures for 2005)
Includes bibliographical references (p.   ) and index.
ISBN-13: 978-0-8139-2626-1 (cloth : alk. paper)
1. Language and languages—Philosophy. 2. Language
and culture. 3. Nihilism (Philosophy) I. Title.
P107.M85   2007
401—dc22
2006025468

Contents

Acknowledgments   *vii*

INTRODUCTION
Discursive Conditions   *1*

ONE
Language, Philosophy, and Sophistry   *13*

TWO
Contributions to a Conversation about the
Conversation of Humanity: Heidegger and
Gadamer, Oakeshott and Rorty   *40*

THREE
Lectures and Letters as Conversation:
Cavell as Educator in *Cities of Words*   *67*

CONCLUSION
Redeeming Words   *99*

Notes   *111*

Bibliography   *115*

Index   *117*

Acknowledgments

I owe thanks to many people who have contributed in various ways to the making of this book. First, to D. Z. Phillips and his colleagues, for their initiative and efforts in organizing the Swansea conference on Rhees's work, and to all those who participated in it. Second, to Rai Gaita, for his invitation to deliver the 2004 Simone Weil lecture, and for his (and his family's) generous hospitality during my stay in Melbourne; to Steve Buckle, for being such a stimulating and well-informed interlocutor and guide during my days in Sydney; and to the Australian Catholic University, for founding and hosting this series of lectures. Finally, to the Page-Barbour Committee of the University of Virginia for inviting me to give the 2005 Page-Barbour lectures; to Jamie Ferreira, Walter Jost, Cora Diamond, and the other members of the departments of Religious Studies, Law, and Philosophy for their unstinting conversation and companionship during my visit to Charlottesville; to Richard Holway, for his painstaking and flexible oversight of the process of transforming the lectures into a book; and to two readers appointed by the University of Virginia Press, for their helpful comments. As always, I also thank Alison, Eleanor, and Matthew for making it possible for me to take advantage of the opportunities that these invitations created.

THE CONVERSATION OF HUMANITY

Discursive Conditions

When I was invited to give the 2005 Page-Barbour Lectures at the University of Virginia, I was told that Mrs. Thomas Nelson Page (who originally established the series in 1907, in honor of her husband and her family) had specified that they might be given in any field of the arts and sciences, that they were to present "some fresh aspect or aspects of the department of thought" in which the lecturer is a specialist, and that they were to possess such unity as to make them publishable in book form by the university. Conscious of the illustrious ranks of those who had preceded me in this role (they include Alfred North Whitehead, John Dewey, Leo Strauss, Northrop Frye, and T. S. Eliot), I asked myself at the moment of delivering my lectures—as I ask myself again now, in prospect of their publication—whether what they contain properly answers to, say acknowledges, the terms of that invitation.

Is the aspect or aspects of philosophical inquiry that they address "fresh"? In one sense, plainly not: as the first lecture aims to suggest, understanding language, human culture, and philosophy in the light of a certain idea of conversation or discourse was first attempted by Plato, and so has decisively marked the Western philosophical tradition from its outset. In another sense, however, as Heidegger insists most explicitly, that attempt constantly finds itself slipping out of philosophical focus, as if endlessly subject to repression; to this extent, it might be thought of not so much as a fresh concern as one that stands constantly in need of refreshment or recovery—as if its original expression has marked the intellectual tradition it helped to found by resisting its own dismissal, hence by demanding that we recall or remember it. It is, I will suggest, one way in which philosophy's origin haunts its present—one form in which the repressed familiar uncannily returns.

Does my theme pertain to philosophy understood as a "department of thought"? Here, again, the answer must be yes and no; and here these lectures register the familiar difficulty in understanding philosophy's relation to other departments of thought in human culture—the fact that, and the reasons why, philosophy both accepts and resists consignment to the ranks of the arts and sciences. This sense of such consignment as a potentially fatal confinement is clearly expressed in philosophy's perennial attempts to picture itself as essentially, necessarily, not on the same level as other arts and sciences: sometimes—as with the picture of philosophy as an underlaborer—this resistance takes on a cast of humility; sometimes—as with the picture of philosophy as the queen of the sciences—it has a more arrogant air. Whether one finds one of these moods more congenial than the other, or rather comes to think that it is the perennial oscillation between the two that best captures philosophy's condition, the condition for their possibility is surely a sense that philosophy can neither simply deny that it has a place in the economy of human culture, nor simply accept that its place is settled—say, as one more member of the ranks, or one more field to be cultivated. Against this background, one might say that my ways of reviving the suggestion that human culture in general, and philosophy in particular, be thought of as possessing a dialogical or conversational structure are in fact another way of putting in question the assumption that philosophy is a department of thought (that is, just one more, or just one among a number of such departments). It would be hard for me to deny that this line of thought will elicit charges of arrogance more easily than it will compliments on humility.

Do my lectures possess the kind of unity appropriate for publication in book form? I cannot, of course, take their actual appearance in the form of a book to settle that question of appropriateness. But suppose we rephrase this aspect of the original invitation as raising the question of how the form of lectures and the form of a book are, can be, and should be related to one another. More specifically, we might ask: what happens to the unity of a discourse when it is transformed from an essentially oral to an essentially written mode of pedagogy? So formulated, this is precisely the topic of my third lecture, which considers the specific response to that question that is developed in Stanley Cavell's *Cities of Words*, which he describes as a book of letters that follows the course of a course of his lectures, and whose epistolary form manifests his solution to the difficulties that such transformations create when the pedagogy is philosophical in genre, and moral (more specifically, moral perfectionist) in content.

In effect, then, my answer to the question of whether these lectures constitute an apt acknowledgment of the terms of Mrs. Thomas Nelson Page's invitation is: it depends on what she, and we, might mean by "fresh," by "department of thought," and by "discursive unity." No doubt this is just the response one would expect from a philosopher to a generous and straightforward invitation. What representative of any other of the arts and sciences would feel the need to tarry over its terms rather than simply act upon them—doing what the invitation asks? More precisely, which would more specifically feel that so to tarry— to see difficulties worthy of thought where all seems clear—is his or her discipline's way of doing what it asks? Is an acknowledgment, in the form of an enactment, of that difference a kind of arrogance, or a kind of humility?

<hr />

Two years before receiving my invitation from the Page-Barbour committee, I was invited to attend a three-day conference at the University of Swansea, which was exclusively devoted to the task of critically evaluating Rush Rhees's posthumous book, *Wittgenstein and the Possibility of Discourse*. Rhees was a student of Wittgenstein's who became one of his most regular philosophical interlocutors; after Wittgenstein's death, he acted as one of his literary executors, taught many of the most influential figures in the brilliant postwar generation of Wittgensteinian philosophers, and helped to give Swansea's philosophy department its distinctive character and consequent impact on Anglo-American philosophical culture more generally. The specific text with which we were concerned is just one of many volumes of material that Professor D. Z. Phillips has managed to extract, edit, and publish from the vast Nachlass of philosophical writings that Rhees produced on a daily basis over the course of a working lifetime, without any apparent concern to make them public. This volume provides a broader context for the thoughts about Wittgenstein's example of the builders' language-game (constructed in section 2 of the *Philosophical Investigations*) that first appeared (much to their author's disquiet) in a famous and controversial article entitled "Wittgenstein's Builders."[1] And what this broader context makes clear is that Rhees's apparently local suspicions of the suggestion that the builders' truncated calls might be worth calling a "complete primitive language" are in fact internally related to his sense of the fate of a primordial philosophical question (namely, What is a language? or What is it to speak?)—a question whose fate is in turn fateful for human culture in general, and philosophy in particular.

For those of us who found it difficult to see exactly why Rhees was so exercised by the builders' inability to have a conversation about their task or their lives more generally, the revelation of this broader horizon—with its particular interweaving of apparently distant themes—through the posthumous publication of this material further raised the stakes of a proper understanding and appreciation of both article and book. For although, among the very small number of those who had attempted to interpret Rhees's concerns, important work by Rai Gaita, D. Z. Phillips, and (most recently) Patrick Rogers Horn had helped to clarify some of the ways in which Rhees's image of a conversation sheds light on the nature of speech and language,[2] they had either not brought out or not properly explained its implications for our understanding of the relation between language, culture, and reality, and hence for philosophy in its struggle with sophistry for a genuine form of self-understanding. And what this new book revealed was that to omit such implications was to omit something utterly central to Rhees's self-understanding.

At the same time, however, the book's publication also intensified the difficulties involved in attaining such a full understanding of Rhees's project; for Phillips's heroic editorial work has also helped to reveal the full idiosyncrasy of Rhees's natural style of philosophical composition (when not even partly informed, or deformed, by the requirements of article-length journal publication). The full manuscript is in reality organized not in terms of premises and conclusions, or in chapters or subsections of chapters (these are editorial constructs), or even in terms of sequences of texts under examination, but rather in terms of a chain of interlinked pronouncements around which the writing endlessly circles, following out new connections between any two of them in order to come again at each from a series of new angles or perspectives. Since I cannot presume on any prior acquaintance with this, or indeed any other of Rhees's posthumous publications, here is a representative sample of the pronouncements that form its skeleton: "To speak is to have something to say"; "To speak is to be capable of growth in understanding"; "The unity of language is the unity of a dialogue"; "Language makes sense insofar as living makes sense"; "Philosophy makes sense insofar as living makes sense"; "Philosophy is discourse about the reality of discourse"; "The reality of philosophy is the reality of language."

These pronouncements deploy no syntactic or semantic complexities, being essentially composed of utterly simple, everyday words, but they are nevertheless essentially oracular, Delphic: they are indicative rather than assertorical, as if posing a riddle whose solution is at once only just beyond our grasp, but which (once grasped) will open new horizons of significance that will have a quality of intense familiarity (conveying a sense of the new as a recombination of the familiar, hence as something of which we need to be reminded). Rhees stands toward them as if toward the remarks of another, as if he is no more certain of what they might mean than we are; he focuses with hallucinatory intensity upon the specific words and phrases that compose them, generating a sense of their almost unfathomable depths and connotations, together with a sense of their mutual implication or invocation. And his essays at self-interpretation, in their crabwise progress or lack of progress or reiterated expressions of despair about the possibility of progress, engender the impression that his discourse is not bound by starting or finishing points that have anything more than a provisional necessity—so that, as readers, we come to interpret ourselves as eavesdropping on a conversation that is without beginning or end.

I hope that it is clear that such writing sets a stark challenge to its readers, and a particularly stark challenge to its philosophical readers; for the essentially oracular invokes the possibility of an authority extraterritorial to reason, or at least the dangers of a cult—with its esotericism, and hence its division of those it addresses into insiders and outsiders. One might even say: it conjures up the threat of sophistry—of emptiness marketed as profundity, an essential hollowness behind the appearance of wisdom, a refusal to acknowledge any genuine accountability for one's words. And yet, it turns out that these oracular words take the threat of sophistry as one of their central topics; and they further claim that if one fails to find a way of meaning them, of standing behind them and taking responsibility for them, then that failure will in fact amount to the triumph of sophistry, and hence the internal overcoming of philosophy. This alone should remind us that there is a difference between writing in such a way as to invite the charge of sophistry, and writing in such a way as to succumb to it—that one might, in

THE CONVERSATION OF HUMANITY

short, have good philosophical reason to write in a manner calculated to cause offense (and not only to philosophers). We might thereby be encouraged to consider the possibility that there is more than one way of taking responsibility for one's words—ways other than those of inference construction and textual exegesis.

The Swansea conference, and the possibilities it offered of conversation with philosophers such as Dewi Phillips, Rai Gaita, and Roy Holland about just such topics, gave me the initial confidence that there were depths to this text that would repay further study; and Rai Gaita's invitation to deliver the 2004 Simone Weil lecture at the Australian Catholic University, first in Melbourne and then in Sydney, gave me the opportunity to present the results of that further study in a particularly congenial and stimulating pair of intellectual contexts. Those results amounted to an earlier version of the material in the first chapter and the concluding third of the second chapter of this book, prompted by an initial sense of the proximities and distances between Rhees's Wittgensteinian work and that of Gadamer, Oakeshott, and Rorty. And partly as a result of the conversations consequent upon my lectures in Australia, it became clear to me that a far more detailed discussion of Heidegger's early work would provide a useful—even a decisive—bridge between these two stretches of material.

For, as I say at the beginning of the second chapter, the extent and precision of the congruence between Rhees's view of these matters and that of the author of *Being and Time* came as a genuine shock to me. Perhaps their shared sense of incalculable indebtedness to Plato should have made this unsurprising; but despite my settled conviction that there must be opportunities for conversation between the prevailing Anglo-American and Franco-German dispensations of philosophy, the disclosure of this particular opportunity—with its linking of a certain task of philosophy with the possibility of authentically individual existence in a genuine culture (as opposed to what Nietzsche might call its philistine simulacrum)—was an unlooked-for gift.

And, as with all such gifts of interrelatedness, I have found that it has reoriented my sense of what is really at stake in both of the bodies of work thereby related—made each at once more familiar and more original, hence more meaningful contributions to the philosophical traditions to which they so antagonistically relate themselves.

It would certainly be no exaggeration to say that, for many philosophers, Heidegger epitomizes the way in which philosophy can succumb to sophistry—in which those supposedly most deeply committed to rigorous, contentful speech and thought can most thoroughly betray that commitment. In Heidegger's case, that suspicion is raised immediately (and for many, decisively) by the nature of the question with which he begins *Being and Time*—the question of (the meaning of) Being. For despite its august philosophical heritage, that term might seem to exemplify metaphysical emptiness, encouraging us to seek out something—some transcendent or transcendental substance or entity—to which the term must refer, rather than recognizing that insofar as it has a function or functions, they relate to non-referential parts and acts of speech (such as the "is" of existence, the "is" of predication, and the "is" of equality). If, however, I am right in thinking that Heidegger's provisional sense of the meaning of "Being" interweaves a certain Kantian conception of the interrelation of ontological conditions with the conditions for human understanding, together with an ancient sense of philosophy as at once a parasite within, and the radicalized fulfillment of, any genuinely human form of life, then his question will have shown itself to be undismissable for any post-Kantian form of modern analytical philosophy.

If one can think of my first and second lectures as articulating the coherence and substance of this vision of language, culture, and philosophy as dialogically unified each from one side of the "divide" between Anglo-American and Franco-German philosophical traditions, then my third lecture focuses on the work of a philosopher for whom these two traditions are always already conversant with each other (and in a way that has itself invited charges of sophistry). This assumption goes together in Cavell's work with the assumption that philosophy and the arts are also conversant with one another, each having its own interest in, and its own ways of articulating and interrogating, matters that are of concern to the other. In *Cities of Words*, the topic of mutual interest is that of moral perfectionism, understood as a dimension of moral thinking that at once underlies and cuts across the traditional division of the kingdom of ethical theorizing between Consequentialism, Kantianism, and Virtue Theory. In Cavell's hands, such perfectionism naturally precipitates a concern with conversation or dialogical discourse, and hence furthers my interest in the notion of discursive unity; but that internal relation in turn retrospectively confirms that Rhees's concern with the reality of language, culture, and philosophy, and Heidegger's concern with the relation of those issues to the question of authentic (which means internally discursive) human existence, are both best understood as modes of perfectionist thinking—one might say, ways of enacting a conception of philosophy as itself possessed of a perfectionist dimension (a conception Cavell himself shares).

These sets of connections could, of course, be further pursued, and in a number of interrelated ways—ways that would each bring out the interrelation of philosophy with other dispensations of the humanities. One might, for example (as was suggested to me during my week in Virginia), explore the relation between Rhees, Heidegger, and Cavell and a cognate notion of dialogical structure in the work of Bakhtin; or one might examine the ways in which the idea of conversation has formed the topic of explicit study in a number of works of art—in the series of *Alien* movies, or in Coppola's film *The Conversation* (matters I was very tempted to broach in place of the study of Cavell that in fact constituted my third lecture).

In the end, however, I felt that the conclusion to the series of lectures that their present publication allows me the time and space to append should acknowledge a dimension of their work that is largely left implicit in the lectures themselves—the relation of these thinkers and their thought to the field of religion. This may be least obvious in the case of Rhees's reading of Wittgenstein, although his perfectionist concern with the meaning or sense of human life and culture implicitly opens upon it, and its oracular form of expression surely does likewise. The issue is more in the foreground with Heidegger (and Gadamer), given the deep indebtedness of Heidegger's thinking about human authenticity to St. Paul and Kierkegaard, and the threatening intimacy between his conception of the discursive unity of Being and the (what he castigates as ontotheological) biblical conception of the unified field of creation. It is a matter of direct, even if passing, significance for Cavell—in part because of his awareness of the existence of religious forms of perfectionism, in part because of his sense that modern philosophy defines itself by the rejection of religious forms of authorization, and in part (as I argue) because of the internal formal relation between his "pedagogical letters" and the Epistles.

The conclusion itself will work out these relations as concretely as I am at present in a position to manage. But it might be worth noting one general reason for taking that relation seriously in this introduction. I asked earlier whether any other of the arts and sciences could be characterized by a simultaneous acceptance and rejection of the idea that it was (just, simply, merely) one of those arts and sciences, one more branch of culture or department of thought—by a tendency to think of itself as *primus inter pares*. It seems to me that theology is one (and perhaps the only) such contender; for the focus of its distinctive discourse is not just one among many possible objects of human discourse but is also simultaneously understood as founding, grounding, or otherwise sustaining the existence and nature of all such topics. The Creator lies beyond or behind—more specifically (in Christian, that is, Incarnational and Trinitarian terms) simultaneously within and without—the unified field of creation. It is, of course, Heidegger's view that theological thinking is peculiarly prone to the errors of ontotheology—that is, to invoking God (understood as a being, even if one with unequaled powers and capacities) as the answer to the question of Being, when Being is not and cannot be just another being (since it is the condition for the possibility of encountering any and every being). But to say that ontotheology is an error does not amount to a condemnation of theology or faith, but rather to the diagnosis of a perversion that it must strive to avoid. And insofar as it does avoid it, then its essentially unstable mode of inhabiting our cultural economy all but declares its uncanny intimacy with philosophy.

ONE

Language, Philosophy, and Sophistry

NAMING, CONVERSING, AND SPEAKING

One of our oldest accounts of the first human use of language, and hence of the nature of what is thereby used as well as the nature of those using it, goes like this:

> And the Lord God said, it is not good that the man should be alone; I will make him an helpmeet for him.
>
> And out of the ground the Lord God formed every beast of the field, and every fowl of the air; and brought them unto Adam to see what he would call them: and whatsoever Adam called every living creature, that was the name thereof.
>
> And Adam gave names to all cattle, and to the fowl of the air, and to every beast of the field; but for Adam there was not found an helpmeet for him.
>
> And the Lord God caused a deep sleep to fall upon Adam, and he slept; and he took one of his ribs, and closed up the flesh instead thereof; and the rib, which the Lord God had taken from man, made he a woman, and brought her unto the man. And Adam said, This is now bone of my bones and flesh of my flesh: she shall be called Woman, because she was taken out of Man.
>
> Therefore shall a man leave his father and his mother, and shall cleave unto his wife: and they shall be one flesh.
> (*Genesis* 2:18–24)

Adam's first use of language is to name the animals; and the author of Genesis might initially seem to imply that naming is an expression of human freedom and power—an imposing or impressing of words onto the world, a way of making the unified field of creation submit to the human will. But this naming is in fact powerless to satisfy the desire that motivates it: it cannot help Adam to conjure up a creature who might be a fit helpmeet, but rather helplessly records her absence. Hence, his linguistic powers in fact amount to a form of receptivity, a willingness to be impressed by the pre-given nature of the world's inhabitants, and to find the appropriate disclosure of that nature in language. This is confirmed when Adam's naming of his newly created helpmeet explicitly embodies his recognition of her nature; and since the name of woman precisely acknowledges that she shares his nature, and hence participates in his possession of and by words, it declares that his aloneness can be overcome only in the company of someone with whom he can speak. Adam and Eve are conversation partners in every sense of that multivocal word: they converse with one another, they are conversant with the Edenic world in which they dwell, they share what Milton calls the "meet and happy conversation" of sexual intercourse, and their next recorded conversation (about the apple, in response to the snake) turns them away from God and out of Eden, converting their very nature into fallenness—a criminal conversation if ever there was one.

Augustine's *Confessions* culminates in a detailed and dazzling reading of the opening chapters of the book of Genesis; so it is very striking that his own opening chapter describes his acquisition of language as if entirely oblivious to the way in which Genesis characterizes words as the currency of conversation rather than the medium of mastery:

> When they (my elders) named some object, and accordingly moved towards something, I saw this and I grasped that the thing was called by the sound they uttered when they meant to point it out. Their intention was shown by their bodily

movements, as it were the natural language of all peoples: the expression of the face, the play of the eyes, the movement of other parts of the body, and the tone of voice which expresses our state of mind in seeking, having, rejecting, or avoiding something. Thus as I heard words repeatedly used in their proper places in various sentences, I gradually learnt to understand what objects they signified; and after I had trained my mouth to form these signs, I used them to express my own desires. (*Confessions*, 1.8)

Wittgenstein famously begins his *Philosophical Investigations* (hereafter cited as *PI*) by citing this passage from Augustine's *Confessions*, and claiming that it gives expression to a particular picture of human language, according to which all words are names, and all sentences are combinations of such names (hence essentially descriptive). He is less explicit about—although not at all insensitive to—the fact that Augustine's autobiographical sketch associates acts of naming with individual acts of possession and aversion, with the isolated expression of desire and the unceasing search for its satisfaction. On Augustine's account, words link individual speakers to individual objects; they are not the medium of conversational exchanges with other speakers, or of educational exchanges with the child in their midst, who is forced to acquire his understanding of those words from observation rather than interaction. And in the mouths of these unsociable elders, naming precedes and is preparatory for moving toward and having, or moving away from and rejecting; it facilitates remaking the world as they would desire it to be—as the seamless complement to their needs and wishes, a way of mastering their world.

Wittgenstein can be understood as devoting the whole of the rest of his book to the business of uncovering the confusions and fantasies that find expression in this passage from Augustine. And one way in which he immediately embarks on that task is by trying to imagine a context in which Augustine's picture of words as names might seem entirely appropriate:

> Let us imagine a language for which the description given by Augustine is right. The language is meant to serve for communication between a builder A and an assistant B. A is building with building-stones; there are blocks, pillars, slabs and beams. B has to pass the stones, and that in the order in which A needs them. For this purpose they use a language consisting of the words "block," "pillar," "slab," "beam." A calls them out;—B brings the stone which he has learnt to bring at such-and-such a call.—Conceive this as a complete primitive language. (*PI*, 2)

Can we? Many philosophers have doubted that we can. They have pointed out that this "language" has no syntax, contains no rules for forming either simple or complex sentences and so has no logical connectives, is incapable of expressing generality, and has only one (imperative) mood, which makes it impossible to speak of truth or falsity with respect to the builders' utterances (since orders can be neither true nor false). However, these worries go with the grain of the Augustinian conception of language that they appear to be resisting; for they focus on the inability of the builders to make true and false claims about reality, and thus presume that the core function of any language is descriptive (worries about the absence of logical complexity in the language are simply a more indirect way of expressing the same anxiety, since logical inference is essentially a matter of the transference of truth from premises to conclusions). And against those worries, we might say that Wittgenstein's fiction certainly provides us with a context of practical activity, a shared vocabulary, ways of using that vocabulary, and criteria for understanding utterances that employ it. Why is that not enough for the builders' calls to merit the label of a complete language, however primitive it may be?

This is where Wittgenstein's student and literary executor, Rush Rhees, famously raised a very different set of anxieties about his teacher's tale.[1] He claims that it gives us no reason to think that any of its protagonists is saying something; and if a

THE CONVERSATION OF HUMANITY

language is the kind of thing in which things are said, in which people speak, then the builders' calls cannot amount to a language. Everything the builders do in Wittgenstein's tale could be done, Rhees claims, by a trained animal, or even by a very simply programmed machine; these builders are simply issuing and reacting to signals.

Understanding an order is not just a matter of responding determinately to a stimulus; it is, at the very least, a matter of understanding what one is being ordered to do. In this particular case, that means that B must not only understand the business into which his own obedient actions fit but also understand why that business might require this action at this point, and hence understand why A issued the order at this point. He must understand that he is building, and what he is building. Hence, if B understands the order, he could also, in principle, issue such orders; we can imagine A's and B's roles being reversed, and so can they. We can further imagine that A might have issued a different order from the one he did deliver—perhaps because there is more than one way of constructing their edifice; and these alternatives might well be something that A and B would discuss. "Why a slab and not a beam here? Wouldn't another pillar be better?"

However, the builders' four calls would not allow for any such discussion; their every utterance is an imperative—questions, suggestions, and assertions are alike beyond them. But then what sense is there in characterizing their utterances as orders if their "language" allows them no other kind of utterance? Orders are what they are in part because they contrast with questions, assertions, and other kinds of speech act. The significance of what speakers say is in part determined by the particular mode of speech they choose to employ from among the alternatives available to them; and hence understanding what is said depends upon understanding that there are such alternatives, and understanding what is implied by any particular one of them. We might, for example, be tempted to wonder why B does not resent always being the recipient and never the issuer of orders. Why doesn't A adopt a more collaborative, conversational tone in their exchanges? And yet Wittgenstein's tale excludes the very possibility of such alternative modes of behavior.

It might be objected that it is perfectly easy to imagine a context in which real builders might use only a small number of words and a single kind of speech act. We need only recall the kinds of generalized noise, bustle, and commotion common to any major building site to realize that efficiency of communication might be much enhanced if a builder and his mate were to go about their complex and sophisticated business using only the simplest menu of short, shouted instructions. But once again, to understand Wittgenstein's tale in this way involves implicitly contextualizing its overt content; it would suggest, for example, that A and B had (or at least could have) discussed their practical difficulties and come up with this intelligent solution, and that they would be capable of adapting their shorthand to newly altered circumstances—changes in the noise level or the nature of the task, for example. In other words, to think of the four calls as meaningful linguistic exchanges involves grasping them as one particular way of getting the job done, and hence as an alternative to other possible strategies, with the choice between them being open to discussion, evaluation, and revision. It is only in the context of a broader linguistic field of this kind that such a primitive set of calls could properly be regarded as a mode of speaking.

It is also worth asking: what makes us think that these people are builders—people engaged in that particular kind of task? We have already seen that to regard B as understanding A's orders is in part a matter of his understanding the activity in which they are jointly engaged; but what exactly is it to understand what one is doing as building? What exactly is being built, and why? Is it a home, a temple, a cinema, a factory, a gymnasium—even a towered city meant to reach heaven? Or are these stones being moved around for another kind of reason—perhaps as part of a sporting contest, or a children's television show, or a form of military training, or a kind of punishment? According to Rhees, what Wittgenstein describes seems more like a game with stones than an episode in a building project—it possesses the air of repetition and self-sufficiency (that absence of external point) commonly met with when children play with wooden blocks, endlessly erecting a pile only to knock it down, and then rebuild it.

In fact, however, the true force of Rhees's point here is not that Wittgenstein has successfully described a game with stones rather than a building project; it is that the content of his tale is not sufficiently substantial to allow us to judge, even in principle, between these two ways of describing what these "builders" are doing. What we know about them is equally consistent with both, and indeed with an open-ended list of other possible characterizations; and that just means that any suggestion that they are doing one as opposed to another of these kinds of activity is essentially empty. What would give content to the judgment that it is a form of building (as opposed to some other activity with stones) is exactly what would give content to the judgment that it is one particular kind of building project (erecting a house as opposed to a temple or a factory): the framing of their words and deeds in a broader social and cultural context in which people not only build but also play games, wage war, and punish criminals, and in which they live in houses, pray, exercise, and watch films. Set in such a context, what exactly these "builders" are doing will be obvious; but apart from it, the assumption that they are doing anything in particular will be entirely empty, and hence so will the assumption that they are saying anything in particular.

SPEAKING, SPEAKING FOR ONESELF, AND GROWTH IN UNDERSTANDING

It is very important to see that Rhees is not rejecting one claim about the essential function of language in order to replace it with another—as if, whereas Augustinian philosophers see the essence of language as lying in naming and description, he sees it as lying in conversation. His point is rather to put in question the very idea that language *has* an essential function. For that idea supports and is supported by a certain methodological assumption. Our understanding of what a language is, and what it might be to possess and understand one, has its home in our everyday life with language—a life of unsurveyable complexity in which speaking is interwoven with an endlessly ramifying field of forms of practical activity, cultural and social institutions, and aesthetic, moral, political, and religious concerns. We might therefore think that the best way to clarify the real nature of language would be to strip away as much of that complexity as possible, if only in our imaginations. After all, words are sounds and marks produced by human beings in response to one another and to the world; so just how simple might our uses of those words be and still be recognizable as words? Does, for example, the use of four words in the context of a simple building project count as an instance of language, however primitive?

Rhees's deepest worry concerns precisely this kind of thought-experimental approach to clarifying concepts. For in his view, it is only in the context of a complex form of life that any particular facet of our ways with words actually amounts to saying one particular thing rather than another, and hence to saying anything at all; to strip away what might appear to be an essentially accidental or anyway dispensable cultural context for those uses of words is in fact to deprive us of any reason to acknowledge what remains as uses of words at all (as opposed to mere signals, or bare noise and ink), and hence to acknowledge those using them as speakers (as opposed to dumb animals or mere machines). This imaginative simplification does not allow us to penetrate a distracting surface show in order to reveal the underlying essence of language; instead, it deprives us of the very substance of the phenomenon supposedly under investigation. The moment we say to ourselves, "We use words in the ordinary circumstances of our lives; could there be such uses in very different kinds of circumstance?" the fatal methodological error has already been made. For our complex life with language is not one thing, and a particular use of a word another—the

THE CONVERSATION OF HUMANITY

former is not an essentially separable circumstance that might vary while the latter is held constant. Rather, for there to be words just *is* for there to be particular ways of using words each with a specific position in, and specific connections with other such things in, our complicated forms of living.

If, then, Rhees is not proposing conversation as an alternative essence of language, or claiming that all uses of language are in fact contributions to conversations, why does he place such emphasis on the human ability to converse? He describes it as a "centre of variation"; in other words, if we try to consider speaking in the light of conversation, if we think of the ways in which speakers are possible participants in conversation, in which non-conversational uses of words resemble and differ from, as well as have a variety of different ways of bearing upon—of hanging together with, leading to and from—the capacity to converse, then we shall be able to appreciate aspects of language, of what it is to speak, and hence of what it is to be a speaker, that we would otherwise downplay or repress altogether.

Let's return to the builders. Suppose we accept that if they really are able to issue and obey orders in the furtherance of their practical goals, then they are also in a position to discuss their project with one another, to have a conversation about it. What might this thought bring to light that is otherwise very likely to be overlooked? First, the fact that they have something to discuss: they are trying to understand, to get clear about, something to do with their building. In order to discuss alternative building strategies, for example, they must both know something about how buildings actually achieve structural stability—how certain points of load-bearing significance might be redistributed within the structure as a whole, how beauty or simplicity might be traded off against efficiency and economy, and so on. But such a discussion would also be guided by a conception of the particular kind of building aimed at, and the particular significance it is supposed to have. Their understanding of how best to resolve certain structural problems and trade-offs may differ according to whether they are trying to build a home, a temple, or a factory, and their understanding of the purpose of each such activity. And the contribution that each speaker will be able to make to such conversations will reflect their own individual experience—not only their know-how as builders but also their views of what constitutes a family home, what a place of worship, and what a place of work, as well as their sense of how doing their own job well affects and is affected by their own views of what is significant in human life. Some builders might see themselves as simply doing a job for a wage; others might see it as a matter of self-respect that they do the job to the best of their ability; others still might see working well as a way of worshipping their god. In this respect, not only might one talk of those who have the necessary basic competence, or even exceptional technical imagination and insight, and those who do not; we might also talk of individuals who have something to say, or something to say for themselves—those who bring something to the conversation from their lives understood more broadly— and those who do not.

One might therefore quite naturally see that the capacity to converse goes together with the possibility of growth in one's understanding (and of course, of the absence of such growth); this would not so much be a matter of adding to one's technical expertise in a given area, but rather of seeing how the various aspects of a given activity might hang together with one another, how one such enterprise might be thought to bear on others, and how one person might see those bearings (both internal and external) differently from another, and why. Such an understanding would manifest itself in an enhanced ability to converse with others, since it would be partly constituted by a deeper grasp of how different individuals might bring their experience and views to a particular conversation, and how one might engage with what they have to say, with a view to understanding it better and perhaps convincing them to see things otherwise. Understanding of this kind is not a matter of accumulating information; it is something whose acquisition and growth calls for the development of certain virtues—a respect for truth, honesty in one's criticisms of others and of oneself, the courage to change one's mind despite the costs involved if a deeper understanding of one's enterprises and oneself demands it, and so on.

What these connections suggest is that conversations are the kinds of exchange that can be shallow and superficial, or deep and penetrating, because they have a concern for truth that goes beyond the accumulation of facts; they involve the desire to get to grips with their subject matter, the recognition that there is something real and valuable to get to grips with, and hence that one can deepen one's understanding of that subject matter, but only in ways that involve a deepening of one's understanding of one's conversation partners, and of oneself. If, then, we consider being a speaker as a matter of being a potential conversation partner, then we might say that to be a speaker is to have something to say (something genuinely responsive both to the reality of the subject matter and to the particular perspectives and concerns of those with whom one is conversing about it) and something of one's own to say (something one is prepared to stand behind, to own rather than to disown—something through which one stakes and declares oneself).

LANGUAGE-GAMES AND THE UNITY OF LANGUAGE

The builders give us an example of what Wittgenstein means by a language-game—a self-contained practice of employing a range of words in ways governed by clear rules and interwoven with forms of practical activity. But it is far harder to pin down the real role or function of language-games in Wittgenstein's philosophical investigations—in part, perhaps, because we mislead ourselves in thinking that they have a single role or function that we might identify. This, after all, is how the term is introduced in the *Investigations:*

> We can also think of the whole process of using words in section 2 [the builders] as one of those games by means of which children learn their native language. I will call these

games "language-games" and will sometimes speak of a primitive language as a language-game.

And the process of naming the stones and of repeating words after someone might also be called language-games. Think of much of the use of words in games like ring-a-ring-a-roses.

I shall also call the whole, consisting of language and the actions into which it is woven, the "language-game." (*PI*, 7)

This "introduction" invokes at least four ways in which the term might be used—to pick out certain ways of teaching children to speak, certain ways in which words are woven into children's games, certain primitive kinds of language, and finally "the whole, consisting of language and the actions into which it is woven." I have argued elsewhere that Wittgenstein means his future uses of the term "language-game" to retain the connotations established by all four of these interrelated initial examples (in particular, the association of language with play, and with childhood);[2] but most commentators have tended to focus on the fourth canvassed way of using the term, and taken it to suggest that Wittgenstein means the idea of a language-game to have a wholly general application to the phenomenon of language.

Perhaps so: but which kind of general application does he envisage? Some of Wittgenstein's later general pronouncements suggest that he thinks we can often dispel our philosophical unclarities about our lives with words by imagining primitive versions of some aspect of them purely as objects of comparison (and hence not as revelations of essence). As he puts it, "Our clear and simple language-games are not preparatory studies for a future regularization of language . . . [but] are rather set up as *objects of comparison* which are meant to throw light on the facts of our language by way not only of similarities, but also of dissimilarities" (*PI*, 130). However, other things that Wittgenstein says about his "language-game" methods have encouraged people to attribute two rather different ideas to him—that to speak is simply to make a move in a language-game, and that language should be thought of simply as a family of such games.

Take one of his most famous methodological remarks:

> When philosophers use a word . . . and try to grasp the *essence* of the thing, one must always ask oneself: is the word ever actually used in this way in the language-game which is its original home?
>
> What *we* do is to bring words back from their metaphysical to their everyday usage. (*PI*, 116)

Taken together, these sentences seem to imply that our actual, everyday uses of words are not simply to be compared with (and hence recognized as essentially distinct from) the uses of words in deliberately simplified, imaginatively constructed language-games, but are rather to be understood as themselves language-games, or at least as sets or arrays of language-games. On this account, ordinary language for Wittgenstein is actually composed of, and so analytically separable into, a very large number of language-games with words: they make up the basic units or building blocks of language, and hence of linguistic competence—not a philosopher's artifact, but rather the *Heimat* of our words, our haven from metaphysics. Such a picture of language and speech is taken to be essential to Wittgenstein's vision of words, and so of philosophy, by many commentators—both those sympathetic to Wittgenstein's work, and those deeply out of sympathy with it. But Rush Rhees's view is that if that picture were correct, then conversation would be impossible, and our very notion of a language would be obliterated.

If understanding the meanings of words really was exhausted by grasping rules for their use, if words were equivalent to pieces in board games, then they could not form the medium of conversational exchanges. For understanding how to converse—how to follow the development of a conversation, how to make a pertinent or telling contribution to it, how to redirect its focus, how to acknowledge the relevance of another's contribution without agreeing with it, how to recognize when it has reached a dead end or when a little further persistence will bring it to an illuminating resting place—understanding all this is not something that can be reduced to the application of a body of rules, or fruitfully compared with learning how to make moves in a game. This kind of understanding is essentially responsive both to the subject matter of the conversation and to the individual contributions of those participating in it; but moves in chess do not have a subject matter, and do not give any individual player the logical room to give expression to what they bring to a game from their experience outside it. If being able to speak involves being able to converse, then it is not just a matter of applying words in accordance with criteria, of making linguistic moves, or of doing things with words.

Rhees is equally concerned to block the thought that language as a whole should be thought of as a collection or family of distinct language-games; but if we are fully to understand this concern, I need to explain another Wittgensteinian term of art. Wittgenstein's notion of a family-resemblance concept is designed to contest the idea that all instances of a given concept must share some feature or set of features with all other such instances. He proposes instead that some concepts might be unified by a complicated network of overlapping and crisscrossing similarities, as any given member of a single family might resemble certain other members in one respect, others in another respect, and still others in no particular respect at all. And he explicitly introduces this idea in order to claim that "language" is a family-resemblance concept, and hence to justify his refusal to answer his interlocutor's request for an explanation of the essence of language—a specification of what is common to everything that falls under that concept.

It might be thought that this claim already commits him to the view that a language is a family of language-games. In fact it does not: for to say that "language" is a family-resemblance concept is not to claim that any given natural language has an internal family-resemblance structure; it is simply to claim that all

THE CONVERSATION OF HUMANITY

the things that we count as "languages" (e.g., English, German, Esperanto, Basic II, the language of fashion, the dance of the honeybee, and so on) have no property or set of properties in common.[3] Nevertheless, since Wittgenstein's exemplary instance of a family-resemblance concept is that of "game," it follows that his own concept of "language-game" is a family-resemblance concept, and so that there is nothing common to everything we count as a language-game (a point already implicit in the multiplicity of examples with which he introduces this term of art in section 7).

Accordingly, if (for the other reasons I canvassed a little earlier) one is already convinced that Wittgenstein envisages a natural language as essentially a collection of language-games, the family-resemblance structure of the concept of a "language-game" might be held to imply that there is something wrong with the question, What does it mean to say something? or What is the unity of language? For why should we expect there to be any such unity in any given collection of language-games, in the fundamentally various ways we speak or do things with words? Wasn't this assumption precisely what led the author of the *Tractatus* astray, compelling him to seek the will-o'-the-wisp of the general form of the proposition, and to attribute to ordinary language the structural unity of a calculus? And doesn't the author of the *Investigations* repeatedly find that philosophical confusions result from a conflation or crossing of language-games—a failure to respect differences of use, and hence of meaning? By contrast, not only does Rhees think that there *is* something that might be called the unity of language; he believes that trying (and failing) to get this unity into focus has been *the* characteristic business of philosophy since its inception, and hence that any conception of language that occludes the question of its unity thereby threatens not only the historical unity but also the deepest concern, and even the ultimate point, of the enterprise of philosophy as such.

This is where the notion of "conversation" as a center of variation finds a second major point of application in Rhees's thinking; for as well as bringing out certain crucial aspects of what is involved in an individual's ability to speak or say something, it provides a way of conceiving of how language as a whole hangs together. Rhees's claim is that the various different forms of human discourse and practice relate to one another in the way that various contributions to a conversation relate to one another. In other words, the unity of language is the unity of a dialogue; the various modes of human discourse about things interlock intelligibly with one another, and the sense that each makes is both constituted by and constitutes the sense of these interconnections. As Rhees puts it: the generality or unity of language is the generality or unity of a form of life.

Part of what Rhees is driving at is already implicit in the ways in which one participates as an individual in specific conversations. Two builders discussing how best to solve a construction problem will bring to bear an understanding not only of construction techniques but also of the economic and political contexts within which they and their employer are working (which option is cheaper, and how much additional expense matters here and now), the kind of building under construction (a house, a church, a factory), and thereby an understanding of the particular activities that go on in such a building, and their relation to other activities in the culture more generally, and so on. The conversation might be about this building project, but it will draw upon the participants' understanding of the bearing of a variety of other domains and concerns upon this particular practical problem; and in the absence of a grasp of those interlocking considerations, the conversation would lose any proper grip on its subject matter.

What this exemplifies is the way in which the various aspects or dimensions of human social life are interwoven with one another. The same phenomenon is also exemplified at what one might call the disciplinary level of culture—the level at which particular domains of human inquiry and activity are rendered systematic and reflective. On the one hand, especially since the Enlightenment and its concern for the autonomy of both individuals and cultural spheres, we have tended to think of the domains of politics, morality, religion, art, history, physics, astronomy, and so on as essentially distinct, possessed of a particular internal logic and purpose that separates them from even cognate domains, and that might itself be the subject of systematic study. On the other hand, whenever human beings try to make sense of a particular phenomenon, we find that any of these disciplines may have a contribution to make to that project.

Suppose we want to understand the phenomenon of global deforestation. We will certainly need to acquire statistical information about its prevalence and rate of acceleration, and thus draw upon a variety of technological and computing resources, and develop a sense of its historical context. If we are to understand why it is happening, we will need to grasp its underlying economic rationale, the ways in which local and international political systems react to it, and in which a given country's climate and geography, social composition, and cultural expectations contribute to it. To determine its costs, we may need to range further, into the realms of botany, biology, and other environmental sciences, into aesthetic, moral, and religious conceptions of its significance—even perhaps into the domains of psychoanalysis, literary criticism, and cultural studies (in order to grasp what kinds of imaginative and psychic meanings have informed our relations to the forest, and hence what—beyond economic and social forces—might be driving us to remove them, as well as what might be lost with their loss).[4]

Like most other issues of interest to us, then, the phenomenon of deforestation will have its historical, political, moral, technological and scientific, social and cultural aspects and implications, and so can be properly understood only by seeing how each of these aspects and implications bears upon the others; and this means that it forms a fit subject for conversation between those well versed in a variety of forms of human inquiry—between historians, scientists, political theorists, sociologists, literary critics, and others. Each participant will bring her own particular understanding and expertise to the conversation; but each can learn from what the others bring to that conversation, and may even alter her understanding of her own enterprise as a result; and each can in principle grasp that the others are capable of making a significant contribution to the task of better understanding the subject matter of the conversation. This is the individually mediated cultural analogue of what Rhees calls the kind of understanding that is capable of growth—of a deepening that finds expression in one's ability to see how things hang together: both the various distinctive modes of human understanding of our life in the world and the various aspects of that life itself.

At this kind of level, Rhees's image of a conversation foregrounds his sense that the various branches of human culture have a bearing on one another, that their distinctive concerns and methods nevertheless can and do interlock intelligibly with each other; and he encourages us to see this as both a reflection and an exemplary instance of the fact that their subject matter— any aspect of reality whatever that bears upon and is engaged by the forms of human life in the world—itself manifests a dialogical unity, each of its aspects having an intelligible bearing on the others. This is why Rhees claims that language makes sense insofar as living makes sense.

PHILOSOPHY, SOPHISTRY, AND EVIL

The full implications of this conversational conception of the unity of language for our conception of philosophy now begin to emerge. For if our forms of life with language, and hence language itself, have a dialogical unity, then so must philosophy, and for two reasons.

The first is that, like any other aspect of systematic human inquiry, philosophy is internally differentiated and unified in a dialogical way. Just as history comprises many branches and subdisciplines, some of which grow toward as well as from branches and subdisciplines of other forms of human inquiry, so too does philosophy. And just as work in one branch of history will bear upon other branches, so work in one area of philosophy will bear upon work in another area; and a deepening understanding of either discipline will manifest itself in an ability to recognize, activate, and elaborate such dialogical relations.

There are, of course, competing conceptions of philosophy that would either resist such a conception of its nature, and hence of what it might be to understand it more deeply, or at least interpret it differently. Some might argue that, with respect to the concept of a person, for example, we should distinguish metaphysical questions from ethical ones—distinguishing the question of what makes a person one and the same over time from the question of how persons should be treated by other persons—and investigate the two with essentially separate tools and resources. We might still think that the results of our metaphysical investigation may have consequences for our moral thinking—as, for example, Derek Parfit has argued that his reductionist view of personal identity will reduce our fear of death. What, however, if—as Nietzsche thought—what constitutes a person as continuous over time, and hence as a single individual, is her ability to make commitments, to be held responsible now for what she said and did in the past—in short, her ability to promise? Then, one might see a rather different kind of relation between the two inquiries; one might argue either that an ethical understanding of persons is prior to a metaphysical understanding of them, or—perhaps more happily—that the two forms of inquiry are not essentially distinct at all (that, as Iris Murdoch claimed, metaphysics is always as much informed by morals as it is capable of informing them).[5]

I have no wish to arbitrate this kind of disagreement here. My point is rather that this is exactly the kind of conversation that philosophers will find themselves engaging in with other philosophers, and that it precisely presupposes that it at least makes sense to see each branch of the subject as having a bearing on others; for the point at issue in this conversation is how best to understand the ways in which those branches interlock (or fail to), and hence how best to understand the essentially dialogical unity of philosophy itself.

From Rhees's point of view, this kind of unity is particularly to be expected in philosophy (more so than in other internally differentiated and dialogically unified disciplines) because of its distinctive mode of generality. One familiar way of understanding the philosophical enterprise is as raising questions about any and every aspect of human forms of life in the world—questions which concern that which is taken for granted within a particular domain of discourse and activity, and hence which cannot be answered from within it without begging the question itself. The philosopher of science might question the validity of inductive reasoning; but since all scientific inquiry presupposes its validity, no scientific result or procedure can possibly answer the philosopher's question. Or the philosopher of history might ask what we mean by the reality of the past; no historical inquiry can answer that question, because it will take the reality of its subject matter for granted.

One might say, then, that philosophical inquiry is essentially parasitic on the existence of the various forms of human understanding of, and inquiry into, reality; it is, in other words, a mode of discourse whose subject matter is the various forms of human discourse. And if, as Rhees claims, those forms of human discourse manifest an essentially dialogical unity, then so must the various forms of distinctively philosophical discourse; if our life with language, and so language itself, have a dialogical unity, then so must the aspect of our (life with) language that takes that life as its distinctive concern. Conversely, if one holds that philosophical discourse has no dialogical unity, that amounts to saying that its subject matter has no such unity; it amounts to assuming that language, and hence our life with language, do not manifest any interlocking intelligibility of the kind that might be a possible object of the kind of understanding that can grow and deepen (or fail to). To adapt Rhees's claim that I cited earlier: if living makes sense, and hence language makes sense, then so must philosophy; and if philosophy does not have this kind of sense, then neither will language, or the human form of life with language.

Hence, Rhees characterizes philosophy as "discourse about the possibility of discourse"—a characterization that has two key implications. First, it acknowledges that philosophy is itself a kind of discourse, one of the many and various ways in which we talk about things; hence philosophy must itself stand in dialogical relations with other modes of discourse. It does not stand outside the dialogical unity that is one of its central preoccupations; rather, what it has to say about that dialogical unity is a contribution to it and an exemplification of it. After all, if it were not, how would it hang together with the other dimensions of our life with language? How otherwise could philosophy have a nonaccidental or noncontingent, a genuinely intelligible, relation to the rest of our form of life?

Philosophy must, then, be a potential conversation partner for other disciplines—such as history, literature, science—not only in the sense that it may have specific things to say about the presuppositions of those disciplines, but also in that they may have something of their own to say about matters that are distinctively of interest to philosophy. This possibility is realized in, for example, the work of Stanley Cavell—when he claims that what is taken up in philosophy as skepticism is taken up in literature as tragedy, or when he finds that psychoanalysis and philosophy each have an interest in manifestations of the human wish to deny the human, or when he sees in the history of Western philosophy a perennial preoccupation with a distinctively perfectionist concept of the self and its world that has its equally perennial moral and religious conceptions. To acknowledge such themes as potential topics for conversation is precisely not to conflate or collapse these various disciplines and modes of discourse, each with its own resources and presumptions, into one another. It is to recognize each of these cultural, ethical, religious, and psychoanalytical traditions as genuinely other to philosophy—that is, as requiring acknowledgment as much for their differences from, as for their resemblances to, a distinctively philosophical perspective.[6] I shall return to Cavell, and hence to this aspect of Rhees's vision of language as conversation, in chapter 3.

But I said that Rhees's characterization of philosophy as discourse about the possibility of discourse had two key implications. The second is that philosophy is concerned not only with the conditions for the possibility of any specific mode of human language but also with the possibility of discourse as such. It cannot be concerned only with particular modes of discourse, as if each might have its distinctive, local kind of sense and yet have no intelligible bearing on any other mode of discourse, as different contributions to a conversation hang together; for each such discourse is what it is partly in virtue of its specific location in the more general field of discourse, and its specific connections with other such modes of discourse. Philosophy must, in short, concern itself with, be struck by, the sheer possibility of speech—the human ability to say, not just any one of a bewildering variety of things, but anything at all about reality.

Rhees takes this aspect of philosophy's responsibilities to be so fundamental because it bears upon a dispute that has marked philosophy from its birth—the contest between philosophy and sophistry. At the beginning of Plato's dialogue the *Republic*, Socrates is confronted by the sophist Thrasymachus, who claims that justice is best understood as whatever is in the interest of the stronger party. One might therefore take him to be offering one among a variety of possible interpretations of our concept of "justice"; and indeed, a little later in the dialogue, Adeimantus and Glaucon develop a recognizably similar view, and thereby induce Socrates to offer a detailed dialectical critique of their stance with a view to developing his own alternative account. But Thrasymachus's position is in fact very different from that of Adeimantus and Glaucon, and in a sense far more logically consistent; for in suggesting that justice amounts to whatever is in the interests of the powerful, he is in fact doubting the reality of justice altogether. If what we talk of as "just" and "unjust" merely reflects the balance of power in a given

social group, then there is in fact no substance or reality to that stretch of our discourse; all that there is to talk about in this domain could be exhaustively expressed in terms of power, and hence language could suffer the loss of the concept of justice altogether without losing its ability to register the reality of things in our human social world.

But even characterizing Thrasymachus as denying that our discourse about justice embodies any reality fails properly to capture the true reach of his skepticism; for it is part of the sophists' position as Plato understands it that they hold the same view of human discourse in general. Their characteristic view that mastery of discourse is a matter of understanding how to achieve rhetorical effectiveness—how to use words to achieve one's goals, that is, to move others to align themselves with the speaker—reduces all speech to a matter of practical efficacy or power (the view that twentieth-century emotivists held of all nondescriptive discourse). In other words, Thrasymachus's view about the true nature of talk about justice is merely a particular application of the general sophistic view about the true nature of human speech as such; it has no reality to it, it embodies distinctions and values to which nothing corresponds in reality, and hence it lacks any genuine substance.

This is why Thrasymachus (unlike Adeimantus and Glaucon) is rightly wary even of entering into a conversation with Socrates: for he knows that in so doing he is merely entering an arena for the exercise of rhetorical power, and he knows that Socrates is a master of such power. So he demands to be paid for his participation; he repeatedly tries to avoid answering Socrates' questions and criticisms, and he tries as far as possible to avoid saying anything himself in defense or elaboration of his position; he also indulges as frequently as possible in more or less vicious forms of abuse—asking why Socrates' nurse allows him to go around spouting drivel, and describing his hollow acceptance of Socrates' successfully argued conclusions as a holiday treat for his interlocutor. Socrates thus characterizes Thrasymachus as springing on the group like a wild beast, as if he wanted to tear them in pieces; he sets his face against the possibility of participating in the epitome of human conversation that is dialectical philosophical discourse because his position amounts to a denial of the possibility of discourse of any kind.

This portrait of the sophist as an abusive wild animal utterly resistant to domestication in discourse is thus not simply a caricature of the sophists' position, a way of making Socrates' victory over his most intimate enemy far too easy; it is a drawing out and rendering concrete of the sophistic view of language as such, and hence of our life with language. To view human discourse with the sophists is to reduce it to the brutish exercise of power, to void it of any genuine substance; it amounts to denying that there is anything to understand in what people say to one another in conversation—to view language as a whole as entirely failing to make any contact with reality. This is more than mistaking a particular appearance for reality, more even than losing one's grip on the very distinction between illusory appearance and reality in some particular domain; it amounts to rendering utterly unreal or empty the distinction between making contact with reality and failing to do so right across the board.

For Rhees, this is the threat contained in any attempt to understand what it is to speak in terms of an analogy with moves in a game, and to understand language as a family of self-sufficient language-games. Such attempts teeter on the brink of characterizing linguistic understanding as a matter of knowing how to do things with words, to achieve certain effects or practical outcomes; and in so doing they risk eviscerating human modes of discourse of any genuine substance, regarding them as akin to moves in a meaningless game rather than ways of being responsive to reality. They thereby doubly deprive philosophy of any genuine substance, by depriving it of its central subject matter (by denying that there is any such thing as human discourse) and by regarding its distinctive brand of dialogue as having no more genuine substance than any other mode of discourse. To present philosophical wisdom as one more commodity for sale in the agora, and to present it to one's paying customers as a matter of mastering rhetorical techniques, is not so much to mistake sham philosophy for the genuine article; it is to lose one's grip on the very idea that there is a real distinction to be drawn in this area. And that not only deprives philosophy of sense; it implies a corresponding lack of sense in language, and in our life with language, altogether. Hence, Rhees at one point claims that sophistry is not so much mistaken as evil; for to take it seriously is to empty human life of meaning or sense.[7]

Rhees does not think that a thoroughgoing sophist will be converted simply by offering him a philosophical account of human discourse as having some bearing on reality. In part, this is because the consistent sophist will deny that any such philosophical account will itself have any reality to it; it will rather be an exercise in rhetorical manipulation. In part, it is because the sophist is not defending a coherent alternative view of thought and language, but rather inhabiting a self-subverting fantasy of them; she believes that she has grasped the truth about discourse, but her view empties the very ideas of discourse, truth, and reality of any content. Hence, one might say that there is no argumentative route from sophistry to a perception of human discourse as genuine; there are only sophistic ways of removing oneself from a life within the reality of human discourse (among which we might count talk of language-games), and hence ways of trying to prevent or discourage people in general, and philosophers in particular, from so exiling themselves.

But how exactly does the idea of language as having the unity of a dialogue or conversation discourage us from such damaging errancies? How does it allow us satisfactorily to acknowledge the reality of discourse? One way that it must avoid is that of suggesting that human culture amounts to one big conversation, hence that our various ways of discursively grasping reality constitute contributions to an overarching discourse that takes as its subject matter Reality as such—Reality as essentially One. We must recall that the idea of conversation at this (or indeed any) level of Rhees's account is a center of variation, not a putative description; and although Plato might have been tempted by such a hypostasization of the Real, Rhees is not.

His thought is rather that the image of a conversation suggests an account of any given mode of human discourse in terms of its own dialogical unity—with the multiple bearings of each branch of that discourse on other branches giving substance to the thought that each individual branch gets a purchase on reality by showing how the purchase it offers hangs together with (that is, is fruitfully intelligible to, and can itself render fruitfully intelligible) the purchase offered by other branches. And the same kind of account can then be given of the relations between these given modes of discourse: their various ways of interlocking with one another substantiate the claims of each to register some aspect of the reality of things.

Once again, we see the contextualizing thought that what centrally constitutes the nature and reality of a given form of discourse is its specific place in the interlocking unity of human discourse as such. In its proper place in this discursive context, each such mode of discourse really is a way of getting to grips with what is real; and apart from it, its claim to be a mode of discourse (and hence to articulate a way of distinguishing reality from illusion, a way of getting at the truth of things and of achieving a growth in understanding) loses its substance. One might say, then, that, for Rhees, all that can be milked out of the idea of Reality as such, Reality as essentially One, is the fact that our modes of discourse are dialogically articulated and dialogically interrelated. Hence, to show that and how those different modes of discourse are so articulated and bear upon one another in such ways just *is* to show that there is genuine reality in the different ways we talk to one another about our world. It doesn't give us good or bad grounds for believing this to be the case; it clarifies what the claim that it is the case—and hence what the possibility of discourse, of language that is open to reality, of speech—in fact amounts to.

The question with which this leaves us is: is this kind of

clarification really enough? Can the idea of conversation as a center of variation for our thinking about language and philosophy really hope to tame the Thrasymachean impulses in us all? I hope to provide more material for constructing an answer to this question in the next two chapters.

TWO

Contributions to a Conversation about the Conversation of Humanity

HEIDEGGER AND GADAMER, OAKESHOTT AND RORTY

The idea that language exhibits dialogical unity, with its companion idea that philosophy is discourse about the possibility of discourse, has not exactly been a central topic of conversation in the analytic and postanalytic dispensations of Anglo-American philosophy over the last century or so. Furthermore, developing this pair of ideas from within Rush Rhees's way of inheriting the work of Wittgenstein is not likely to alter this state of affairs: for Wittgenstein's way of philosophizing (early and late) has far too rapidly transformed itself for many contemporary philosophers into a curiosity in the history of their subject, and even among the small band of those still inclined to take present guidance from Wittgenstein, there are few who regard Rhees's version of Wittgenstein as anything other than obscure and eccentric. I have done what I can to dispel this obscurity in the previous chapter; in the present one, I will attempt to dissipate its appearance of eccentricity.

In part, this will involve collating evidence for thinking that the ranks of those eccentric to mainstream Anglo-American philosophy in this respect are rather larger than might at first appear—both for better and for worse with respect to Rhees's sense of things. But before taking on that task, I want to demonstrate that Rhees also shares his sense of things with at least two of the most toweringly influential figures in twentieth-century French and German philosophy—Heidegger and Gadamer.

This could hardly have come as more of a shock to Rhees (who evinced precisely no interest in that side of the contemporary philosophical mind) than it did to me; for despite working for many years on a variety of ways in which Wittgenstein and Heidegger seemed to me to be unrecognized conversation partners, discovering this particular connection between their ways of doing and conceiving of philosophy was an unlooked-for gift—a cause of pleasure, certainly, but in precise proportion to my sense of surprise. Perhaps, however, one can only find the familiar on the other side of a conversation if one is prepared to maintain one's sense of the otherness of that side in the face of numerous temptations to proclaim its (essentially premature) overcoming. That, at least, will be the wager of this chapter.

THE CONVERSABILITY OF BEING

It is often assumed that the question with which *Being and Time* (hereafter cited as *BT*) (and thus the whole of Heidegger's thinking) is concerned is the question of Being. We might therefore naturally expect him to tell us a little more at the outset concerning the subject matter of this inquiry; to what exactly does he take the term "Being" to refer? In fact, however, it is central to Heidegger's understanding of our present circumstances not only that we have no answer to this question but that we are no longer even perplexed or bewildered by that lack. Hence he defines his first task as that of "reawaken[ing] an understanding for the meaning of this question" (*BT*, foreword), and specifies his aim in *Being and Time* as that of concretely articulating the question of the meaning of Being. So he can hardly begin his book by offering a neat, clear answer to the very question at whose proper articulation it is the ultimate purpose of that book to arrive; to get the question properly posed will be achievement enough.

On the other hand, Heidegger also thinks that all of us necessarily inhabit an implicit, inarticulate understanding of Being; simply to grasp that "the sky *is* blue" or that "I *am* merry" is already to make use of the very term in question, even if one cannot give adequate expression to what one understands in so doing. Moreover, Heidegger believes that no human inquiry can altogether lack a provisional understanding of its subject matter; how, after all, could one even begin to seek something without some kind of grasp—however superficial or prejudiced or otherwise questionable—of what is sought? Hence, he must be in a position to give his readers some preliminary grasp of what he means by "Being," and in fact he does precisely that.

> In the question which we are to work out, *what is asked about* is Being—that which determines entities as entities, that on the basis of which entities are already understood, however we may discuss them in detail. (*BT*, 1.25–26)

The determination referred to here is twofold: to understand an entity as an entity is to understand it as existing (as opposed to not existing) and as having one particular kind of nature or essence (as opposed to another kind). Hence, Being is not itself a being—not one more kind of entity we might understand. We cannot grasp Being except insofar as we grasp an entity in its Being; but since to grasp an entity as the entity it is—that is, to understand it—just *is* to grasp it in its Being, then whenever we comprehendingly encounter any kind of being we also grasp Being. In short, "[e]verything we talk about, everything we have in view, everything towards which we comport ourselves in any way" (*BT*, 1.26) involves and exemplifies our understanding of Being.

One might then conclude that Being is the most universal concept, and that its use is to pick out the most general class or genus of entities. The idea would be that we arrive at our concept of Being as if by progressive abstraction from our encounters with specific beings: from our encounters with cats and dogs we abstract the concept of "animality"; from animals, plants, and trees we abstract the idea of "life"; and from living beings, minerals, and so on, we abstract the idea of that which every entity has in common—their being.

Heidegger rejects this model of the universality of Being for two reasons. First, because membership in a class is standardly defined in terms of possession of a common property, but the "members" of the "class" of beings do not manifest such uniformity. The being of numbers does not intuitively seem the same as the being of physical objects, which in turn differs from the being of values, emotions, and so on. Second, and more importantly, definition by genus and species works by distinguishing a species as one variant within a larger class—as animals are understood as one, and plants as another, specific kind of living being. But if Being is at the very top of the family tree of concepts constructed by such definitions, then necessarily there is no more general class within which it can be differentiated as one distinctive species among others. In other words, Being necessarily resists definition in this as in any other way appropriate to the definition of beings; Being is not a being, and neither is it a type or property of beings. It is neither a subject of predication nor a predicate.

But in rejecting this model of Being's universality as a concept, Heidegger is not rejecting its universality as such. He means rather to make us ask: if not in the universality of a class or genus, then in what does Being's universality consist? He mentions in passing Aristotle's idea that this universality is transcendental—that is, that it consists in a unity of analogy, what Heidegger calls the "categorial interconnectedness" holding between the various ways in which beings can be grasped as existing and as manifesting a particular kind of existence. (He might equally well have cited the unified field of creation in the book of Genesis, as Adam opens himself to it, with the specificity of each creature disclosed against the background of their common creatureliness—their relation to God as Creator). And Heidegger gives this alternative model of Being's universality a fuller specification when he analyzes what he calls the ontological priority of the question of Being.

He begins by pointing out that our pretheoretical comprehension of the phenomena of everyday life is never absolutely final or complete, but rather always capable of being further refined or developed, even of being radically revised or reconceived; in this sense, our everyday grasp of things is inherently open to question. I may have a good understanding of our cat, Jemima, and hence of certain kinds of animal life, and nonetheless be deeply surprised on occasion by something Jemima does; I may be forced to revise my sense of the general character of cats by the particular temperament of my neighbor's animal; and of course, such surprises might lead me to pursue a more systematic understanding of that species, and of animal life more generally. We might accordingly think of disciplinary practices such as biology, zoology, and anthropology (Heidegger calls them ontic sciences) as what result from making an issue of this everyday understanding; we rigorously thematize it with a view to systematically interrogating it, and develop thereby a body of knowledge which may surpass or even subvert our initial understanding, but which is made possible by it and which is no less open to further questioning.

After all, what we learn reveals what we don't yet know; it orients our attempts to acquire that further knowledge; and it may also lead us to question the assumptions that governed our initial theorizing. Moreover, everything we come to know in this manner takes for granted certain basic ways in which this ontic science demarcates and structures its own area of study—conceptual and methodological resources that can themselves be thematized and interrogated (when, for example, biology was revolutionized by Darwinian theories of natural selection, or physics by relativity theory—or when a philosopher of science inquires into the validity of inductive reasoning). Such inquiries concern the conditions for the possibility of such scientific theorizing, what Heidegger calls the ontological presuppositions of ontic inquiry; and whether one inquires into them as a practitioner of the discipline or as a philosopher, the subject matter could not be within the purview of a purely intradisciplinary inquiry (which would necessarily presuppose what is here being put in question). It is, in short, the business of philosophy.

The object of investigation here is what Heidegger calls a

regional ontology; every region of ontic knowledge presupposes one, and thus invites this kind of philosophical questioning. And in the familiar way, the results of each such kind of questioning themselves provoke further inquiry: given that each ontic region discloses an ontology, the relations between the various regional ontologies inevitably become a matter for philosophical inquiry. For on the one hand, each ontology will differ from others, as each ontic region has its own distinctive nature. But on the other, each region may open up onto cognate regions (as chemistry might shed light on biology and zoology, or as Heidegger thinks theology has deformed anthropology, psychology, and biology [*BT*, 10]), thus revealing that its ontology bears upon those others; and of course each regional ontology is an ontology—each performs the same determinative function with respect to its region (determines the Being of a certain range or domain of beings), even if differently in each case. How, then, is this synthesis of categorial diversity and categorial unity to be understood? What is it for beings to be? This is the question of fundamental ontology.

The similarities between this picture of the economy of human knowledge and that of Rush Rhees are striking; for Heidegger is here analyzing the universality of Being on three interrelated levels, and picturing the articulations within and between these levels, in terms very congenial to those I laid out in my first chapter in terms of language. First, there is the internal articulation of philosophy, or ontological inquiry. To engage properly in any regional ontology, one must acknowledge not only that region's distinctiveness but also its context—the way in which its ontology is located among and hence related to others, as well as the way in which the diversity-in-unity of regional ontology invites the question of fundamental ontology (since to thematize that diversity-in-unity just *is* to ask the question of fundamental ontology). Hence, any authentically penetrating exercise of philosophy in any of its regions must also bear in mind its place in, and hence its bearing upon, the broader articulated unity of philosophical inquiry as such. In short, there can be no properly rigorous philosophy of science or philosophy of literature in the absence of a properly rigorous inquiry into the question of the meaning of Being; and to inquire into that question necessarily involves reflecting upon the diversity-in-unity of philosophy.

The second level concerns the ontic sciences upon whose existence and nature distinctively philosophical inquiry is focused. Philosophy is thus, just as Rhees pictures it, parasitic upon the existence of ontic sciences; hence, insofar as regional ontological inquiries hang together with one another in the articulated unity of philosophy (qua intellectual discipline or tradition), then so must the ontic sciences from which those inquiries take their bearing and motivation. Philosophy makes sense (can be seen to hang together as an intelligible whole) only insofar as regional ontologies do so; and for regional ontologies to hang together just is for individual ontic sciences to do so. Their results hang together internally (making it possible to form coherent bodies of knowledge, as opposed to accumulations of purely local data) and externally (insofar as the understanding they systematize has a bearing upon other such forms of understanding—whether by complementing, qualifying, challenging, or otherwise putting it in question).

If the ontic sciences did not manifest such an articulated unity, then to precisely that extent the idea that reality is an articulated unity would lack any genuine substance; for each regional ontology is not only the basis upon which we construct an understanding of the entities of a particular ontic domain but also that which determines those entities as the distinctive kind of entities they are. The fact and nature (the Being) of ontology is thus Janus-faced in the familiar Kantian way, looking at one and same time toward our mode of comprehension of things and toward the nature of the things thus comprehended. In this respect, it reflects Heidegger's provisional understanding of Being, which refers both to that which determines entities as entities and to that upon the basis of which entities are understood. For of course, if we really do understand entities, then we understand them as they really are. And this means that to think of the question of Being as a genuine question (which means to think of philosophy as a genuine mode of understanding) is to think of our ontic sciences as genuine modes of understanding—as ways of disclosing how things really are, getting at the truth of things; it is to think of them as discursive articulations that are also articulations of reality.

The third level of Heidegger's picture concerns the domain from which both ontic knowledge and ontological inquiry emerge, the domain embodying those pretheoretical modes of questioning comprehension whose reflexive radicalization generates the systematic forms of human understanding of the world—the domain of everyday human existence: the domain of Dasein. For, of course, the construction and pursuit of ontic and ontological knowledge is itself an achievement of human beings, hence an aspect of their comprehending, questioning mode of existence. And while such modes of comprehension might embody radical revisions and subversions of our pretheoretical grasp of things, they must also be essentially continuous with that understanding: they must be made possible by it and the resources it makes available; and the ways in which the various aspects of this understanding implicitly hang together must be such that their rigorous thematization is possible in an articulated and unified way. In short, if philosophy makes sense only if ontic science makes sense, then both make sense only insofar as the everyday ways in which Dasein grasps and interrogates its world make sense. Thus, for Heidegger as much as for Rhees, the question of whether living makes sense, the question of whether our ways of understanding the world have any genuine substance, and the question of the meaning or point of philosophy have to be seen as three internally related questions, even as three aspects or dimensions of one and the same question: the question of whether the human form of life has sense or meaning.

This is why Heidegger organizes his characterization of the phemonenological method—that is, his way of approaching the question of the meaning of Being—around the idea of the "logos," whose basic signification he specifies as "discourse." This refers to the capacity to disclose the reality of something; "in discourse, so far as it is genuine, what is said is drawn from what the talk is about, so that discursive communication, in what it says, makes manifest what it is talking about, and thus makes this accessible to the other party" (*BT*, 7.56). The connection between discourse and conversation or dialogue (implicit in the German term *Rede*) is here made explicit; it contains the idea that the discourser is both receptive to the way things really are and receptive to others' best attempts to make manifest the way things are. On this understanding of discourse, its point is always to apprehend what is there to be apprehended, and it is always open to the apprehension of others; hence it is always open to the possibility of being put in question either by the phenomenon or by others' apprehensions of it, but always with a view to deepening our collective apprehension of what is there to be understood. And by the same token, of course, it is always vulnerable to failing to do so. My discourse might subordinate the way things are to the way I want or take them to be, and to the need to conform to what others want or take things to be; and our conversational interactions might thereby float further and further away from what is there to be disclosed, perhaps even to the point of losing touch with the very idea that there is anything real to be disclosed, and hence with the very idea that our discourse has any substance or reality.

It is little surprise, then, that Heidegger thinks of his phenomenological project as most fundamentally opposed to the threat of sophistry. This is underlined by his decision to begin *Being and Time* with a quotation from Plato's *Sophist*, which concerns the efforts of the Stranger from Elea to define the nature of sophistry. This effort ultimately results in the claim that sophists are makers of appearances which are not likenesses (mere semblances, as Heidegger would put it)—a claim to which the sophist is imagined to respond by pointing out that since one cannot say or think that which is not, then this definition itself says nothing: in other words, it is itself an instance of sophistry, not a characterization of it. It is this objection that generates the famous discussion in the second half of the dialogue concerning whether and how one can say or think that which is—Heidegger's question of Being, the question of fundamental ontology. The structure of Plato's dialogue thus reinforces Heidegger's conviction that any adequate response to the sophist must involve taking seriously the question of the meaning of Being—that what sophistry threatens to dissolve is not just the reality of philosophical discourse, but the capacity of language to represent reality altogether (to say of anything whatever either that it is, or that it is not). The sophist doubts the reality of discourse as such; the philosopher aims to account for, or rather to recount, and thereby to acknowledge, that reality both within and without philosophy.

Heidegger's phenomenological model of philosophical inquiry as discursive is thus also intended to model all forms of the distinctively human questioning comprehension of reality—pretheoretical, ontic, and ontological. It depicts them as essentially discursive, hence conversational and dialogical; in this respect philosophical dialogues about Being and its meaning merely radicalize Dasein's distinctively discursive apprehension of phenomena as such, amounting in effect to a discourse about the very possibility of discourse—a discourse in which discursivity as such, and hence both the intelligibility of our ways of apprehending reality and the intelligibility of the reality we thereby apprehend, becomes the object of our discursive apprehension.

This is why Heidegger's inquiry into the meaning of Being takes Dasein as the object of its interrogative apprehension. Since Being is always and only encountered as the Being of some being or other, any such inquiry must choose some particular being to interrogate; and Heidegger chooses Dasein for two reasons. First, because Dasein is his name for the Being of the being who inquires, and no specific inquiry can truly understand its own best possibilities unless it first understands what inquiring as such involves, which must involve understanding the Being of the being who can ask questions. Second, because Dasein is that being who can encounter any and every entity (including itself) in its Being—for whom Being in all of its forms is an issue, a matter of questioning comprehension; hence, to grasp the Being of Dasein would be to grasp what it is to understand all beings in their Being, and one cannot grasp what it is to understand Being (grasp that which permits Dasein to take the Being of beings as its object) without grasping what is thereby understood (grasping what it is for Being, in every one of its ways, shapes, and forms, "to be").

Heidegger's existential analytic of Dasein is thus both an essential preliminary to fundamental ontology and a way of doing fundamental ontology; it is both a means to an end and the end itself. But what makes this so is his picture of Dasein as the unifying existential ground of all possible forms of discourse. The human way of being is not just the origin and condition for the possibility of all forms of discursive understanding; its articulated unity as a being (its Being), the articulated unity of the discursive fields of our culture, and hence the particular articulated unity of philosophy, stand or fall together. They are simply different ways of disclosing the same phenomenon, the categorial interconnectedness of Being. And since Heidegger, like Rhees, sees this diversity-in-unity on the model of a conversation, then he is implicitly conceiving not just of Being, and of philosophy, but of the Being of Dasein itself as comprehensible only in those terms—quite as if Dasein's distinctive way of being is to converse (with its world, with other Dasein, and with itself).

THE CONVERSABILITY OF DASEIN

Two pivotal discussions further into *Being and Time* confirm and flesh out this intuition; and both concern the sense in which the Being of Dasein is both Being-oneself and Being-with—in other words, with Heidegger's intuition that Dasein's way of relating to itself and its way of relating to other Dasein are not only individually constitutive of its way of being but also mutually determining. What he emphasizes for the most part in chapters 4 and 5 of division 1 is the fact that, and the ways in which, this mutual determination typically takes an inauthentic form—the form of "das Man," the "they," the one, the neuter. Here is a flavor of Heidegger's characterization of this average everyday form of human being:

> In utilizing public means of transport and in making use of information services such as the newspaper, every Other is like the next. This Being-with-one-another dissolves one's own Dasein completely into the kind of Being of "the Others," in such a way, indeed, that the Others, as distinguishable and explicit, vanish more and more. In this inconspicuousness and unascertainability, the real dictatorship of the "they" is unfolded. We take pleasure and enjoy ourselves as *they* [one] take pleasure; we read, see and judge about literature and art as *they* see and judge; likewise we shrink back from the "great mass" as *they* shrink back; we find "shocking" what *they* find shocking. The "they," which is nothing definite, and which all are, though not as the sum, prescribes the kind of Being of everydayness. (*BT*, 27.164)

The "they" presents every judgment and decision as its own, and thereby deprives or disburdens Dasein of what Heidegger calls its answerability—of any conception of the judgments, actions, and reactions that make up its existence as being its own judgments, actions, and decisions, its to own, for which it can be held accountable, and through which it might realize a genuinely individual life, a life in which its selfhood might find proper expression. To account for one's projects by saying "that's just what one does, that's what is done" is to stand to one's projects as ones to which there is no alternative; hence engaging in them is not grasped here as genuinely a choice—a choice between alternatives. In this respect, to live in the mode of "das Man" is to repress or deny the fact that the reality, the form, and the content of our existence are something for which we are responsible, to which intelligible alternatives always exist, and hence whose continuation is implicitly a choice against those alternatives—something for which we are, always, answerable. And to repress or deny that fact is not to remove it; it is to confirm it.

But it is not that Dasein's individuality is lost in or subjected to the individuality of specific Others or groups of Others; for insofar as those Others are also part of "das Man," they must lack genuine individuality themselves. They are no more distinguishable from ourselves than we are from them. In this sense, "das Man" is not a kind of communality but rather an absence of genuine communality—a collective hallucination of human community; if the individuals within it cannot say "I," then the collection of those individuals cannot say "We." As Heidegger expresses it, "[E]veryone is the other, and no one is himself" (*BT*, 27.164)

The manifestation of this mode of relating to others to which Heidegger gives the closest attention is—perhaps unsurprisingly—that concerning discourse; for Heidegger, the "das Man" mode of discourse is idle talk (*Gerede:* chatter, chitchat). In contrast to the authentic case, when what one says is genuinely open to its subject matter and to correction by the discourse of others equally open to that subject matter, in idle talk what one judges to be so is determined by what is said about what is so. Things are so because one says so; what is said to be the case determines what one says is the case, and thus reinforces the authority of what is said over how things actually are, to the point at which "conversation" becomes a matter of repeating what is said to one another, and our ability to disclose reality takes the form of closing off—closing off not only the reality of the supposed subject matter but increasingly the very idea that there is an independently given subject matter to which our discourse is meant to be subordinate, and in relation to which one speaker's discourse might contest or otherwise question the other's.

Such a deformation of the human capacity for discursive understanding hangs together, in Heidegger's account, with what he calls "curiosity" and "ambiguity." The sheer repetitiveness of idle talk, together with its sense that the underlying reality of the subject matter has been definitively determined, engenders a curiosity for something new to talk and think about; but since its inhabitants will immediately see that there is only one way to talk and think about this new subject, curiosity will seek yet more novelty, which will yield few returns of genuine interest before going on to newer novelties, and so to an accelerating process of distraction—a constant uprooting. In this context, we will have neither the time nor the space to distinguish between a genuinely deep and a superficial understanding of something. Superficial understanding will pass for deep, and deep understanding for superficial, which will leave us increasingly unclear whether another's discourse is penetrating or merely eccentric, and hence increasingly unable to distinguish someone who has something of his own to say in a conversation from someone who has nothing to say. And these ambiguities will proliferate until the very distinction between shallow and deep, with respect to our discursive understanding of the world, and hence the very idea of reality as having the kind of integrity, complexity, and depth to which a genuine understanding might penetrate, lose their grip.

It is not hard to find examples of this kind of discourse in our everyday experience. In fact, it can sometimes be hard to find anything other than idle talk in what passes for the conversation of our culture. The night before writing these sentences, I listened to an evening news bulletin from the BBC. Its lead item concerned a government bill revising the legal constraints on the validation of living wills. The first reporter spent five minutes weaving together short remarks by spokespeople for contending moral and religious views about euthanasia, thus constructing the simulacrum of a conversation, without ever explaining the nature of the proposed legislation and thus without ever demonstrating any real connection between that legislation and the topic of his "conversation." A second reporter focused on the discontent of MPs, who were not given a free vote on what they saw as a matter of conscience, without ever explaining why the government had decided not to treat it as such a matter (essentially, because the bill modified existing provisions rather than introducing any legal novelties); and he presented his information to us in the familiar way, via a scripted exchange with the presenter of the bulletin, quite as if we viewers were eavesdropping on a real conversation in which people were trying to get clearer about its subject matter. Another item concerned a newly constructed road bridge in France: the camera observed the reporter and the bridge's English architect agreeing with one another about how cleverly its bulk, laid out before them, vanished into the landscape, while we saw that in fact its presence made the landscape vanish. A third concerned a display in the Tate Modern galleries of the work of young men and women from areas of great social deprivation in London; it focused in particular on a painstakingly accurate reconstruction of one young man's filthy, dilapidated bedsit accommodation. Their presence in the galleries was hailed as a validation of their membership of society; "Now they have been given the respect they deserve," one woman commented. But no comment whatever was made concerning the claims of this work to be art, and hence its claim on the museum as a scene for the preservation and display of art as opposed, say, to its ability to dispense social justice. And I watched this bulletin until its end, and will no doubt watch the same channel's bulletin on nights yet to come. Stanley Cavell's term for this cultural condition is "amentia":

> [T]he degree to which you talk of things, and talk in ways, that hold no interest for you, or listen to what you cannot imagine the talker's caring about, in the way he carries the care, is the degree to which you consign yourself to nonsensicality, stupify yourself. (Of course your lack of interest may be your fault, come from your own commitment to boredom.) I think of this consignment as a form not so much of dementia as of what amentia ought to mean, a form

of mindlessness. It does not appear unthinkable that the bulk of an entire culture, call it the public discourse of the culture, the culture thinking aloud about itself, hence believing itself to be talking philosophy, should become ungovernably inane. In such a case, you would not say that the Emperor has no clothes; in part because what you really want to say is that there is no Emperor; but in greater part because in neither case would anyone understand you. (*Claim of Reason*, 95)

But Heidegger's view is that Dasein's mode of Being-with-Others is internally related to its mode of self-relation; and we have not yet seen how idle talk might find its complement (and so, of course, its contrary) in Dasein's way of relating to itself. In division 2 of *Being and Time*, Heidegger presents authenticity as a matter of Dasein's listening to the voice of conscience, and thereby invokes a picture of the self discoursing with itself (or failing to); but he specifies this authentic internal conversation as being "solely and constantly in the mode of keeping silent" (*BT*, 56.318). How does this disrupt the idle talk of the they-self?

Heidegger's view is not that the voice of conscience has no specific content; it is rather that its call always goes beyond its specific content. More precisely: in addressing us with specific guidance about our concrete situation, and thereby addressing us as the occupant of that situation (with specific cares and commitments), it implicitly addresses us as beings capable of and condemned to such situatedness—that is, as beings whose Being is an issue for us, and for whom individuality is a possibility. This dimension of the voice of conscience must, therefore, be essentially nonspecific; it must say nothing, because it does not disclose us as subject to some particular demand, but rather discloses the fact that we are the kind of being who is subject to demand, that our existence as such is something for which we are answerable. And this is why the silent voice of conscience can disrupt the they-self; for it manifests the fact that Dasein is responsible for its existence, that it has a life to own, and that it typically disowns it—to the point at which it represses the very idea of its life as capable of being its own.

The silence of the voice of conscience thus articulates Dasein's essential failure to coincide with itself, its not being itself; the state in which it finds itself is not, is never, all that it is or could be (since that situation might have been otherwise, and is anyway a situation within which it must choose how to go on), and so its present state is never something with which it can fully identify or to which it can be reduced. It is always, in this sense, uncanny or not-at-home. Authenticity is a matter of living out the knowledge of this essential non-self-identity—the essential gap between what it is and what it might be, between its existential actuality and its existential potential. Hence, inauthenticity must be understood as a matter of living as if one coincided with oneself—as if what one currently is and does is simply what there is to be and do, as if the course and continuation of one's existence is fated or necessary, as if one's existence really were entirely lacking in self-differentiation.

In the light of Rush Rhees's work, one might put these matters in the following way. The voice of conscience indicates that, beyond any particular demands the self might address to itself, it is essentially a being capable of addressing itself from itself— a being whose nature is such that its present state is always open to question from the perspective of a state that it might (although it does not yet) occupy, a being for whom to live is a matter of asking and answering oneself about, hence conversing with oneself about, how to live. The fact, form, and content of one's existence are a possible topic of internal conversation only because Dasein's actuality and its potential do not coincide with one another; it is this non-self-coincidence that articulates its essentially dialogical internal structure.

Dasein's differentiation of itself from itself thus engenders (as it were) two perspectives that any self can take upon itself, and one's way of existing is determined by the way in which one manages the relation between those two perspectives. Either the perspective of one's attained state eclipses that of one's unattained but attainable state, or one's attainable state provides a potentially critical perspective on that provided by one's attained state; in the former case, there is no room for any genuine inner dialogue, but in the latter the self can really speak to itself because it is speaking from beyond itself. As Heidegger expresses it: "The call [of conscience] comes *from* me, and yet *from beyond me*" (*BT*, 57.320).

We can thus see a fundamental discursive complementarity between Dasein's authentic and inauthentic modes of Being-with and Being-oneself. In authenticity, insofar as Dasein actualizes its capacity to be other to itself, it actualizes its capacity to have something of its own to say to others, and to take what others have to say as potentially other than what it has to say, hence as potentially expressive of their individuality, and hence as the contributions of potential partners in a genuinely open conversation. In inauthenticity, Dasein's repression of its answerability to itself corresponds to the way in which the sovereignty of idle talk dissolves each Dasein into the other, destroying the differentiation between self and other without which conversation is impossible. One might say: the self's otherness to itself and the self's otherness to other selves, hang together. Dasein's conversability is at once inner and outer—either we have neither, or we have both.

As a consequence, a self that achieves genuine otherness to itself is one whose sheer existence can disrupt the sovereignty of the they-self. For those who exist in the mode of "das Man" do so by, in effect, mirroring one another's lack of self-differentiation and thereby reinforcing it. But when such a Dasein encounters an authentic other, that other cannot confirm Dasein in its anonymity by mirroring it, and she prevents Dasein from relating inauthentically to her. For Dasein could mirror another who exists as self-differentiated and self-determining, and who relates to others as genuinely other, only by relating to her as genuinely other, which means relating to itself as other to that other—that is, as a self-differentiated, self-determining being. The authentic Other thus awakens otherness in Dasein itself.

The relation that other establishes with Dasein exemplifies a mode of Dasein's self-relation—a relation to itself as other; it exemplifies the otherness from, in, and of which the voice of conscience speaks, but it can only do so insofar as it refrains from conflating what it has to say for itself with what the other has to say for itself. It must therefore differentiate the otherness of its own existence from the otherness of the other's existence. In speaking to and for the other's repressed otherness to itself, it must never claim to speak as that otherness, to occupy its place; for that would simply be to subject the otherness of the other to further repression.

One can therefore see why Heidegger wants, on the one hand, to declare that "the call [of conscience] undoubtedly does not come from someone else who is with me in the world" (*BT*, 57.320) and, on the other, to acknowledge that "Dasein can become the conscience of Others," and that the voice of conscience is "the voice of the friend whom every Dasein carries with it" (*BT*, 34.206). The ambivalence in this idea of friendship—with its inversion of Aristotle's image of the friend as another self—is perhaps unavoidable; for Heidegger's settled view seems to be that Dasein's way of relating to itself is a kind of Being-with, and that Being-with(-others) is a kind of Being-oneself. And to picture the self as essentially the capacity to be befriended (by itself as by another) means depicting Dasein as not simply the existential ground for the conversational unity of pretheoretical, ontic, and ontological discourse, as we saw earlier; now we can see that, as this existential ground, it has the articulated unity of a conversation. Dasein is not just the locus and the precondition for the conversation of humankind; it is itself, because humankind is, a kind of enacted conversation.[1]

THE CONVERSABILITY OF THE PAST

I shall return to this perfectionist moral or spiritual dimension of human existence, understood in terms of an essentially conversational mode of being, in the third chapter. But now I want to turn to Hans-Georg Gadamer's work on the hermeneutic structure of human understanding; for this project, following Heidegger and his lifelong struggle against the sophists, repeatedly adverts to the model of conversation, in terms that align him decisively with Rhees's project; but he brings out even more starkly than his teacher the essentially historical dimension of this model.[2]

Gadamer's orienting question is how is it possible for us to come to understand a text that reaches us from the (sometimes very distant) past. He points out that our sense that there is an insuperable problem here derives from the assumption that the necessary historical distance between the text, its author, and its original audience (on the one hand) and us attempting to read it in our present social and cultural context (on the other) constitutes a daunting barrier to understanding. After all, one might think, it ensures that the author's intentions may be entirely beyond our reach; it forces us to grapple with the particular linguistic, generic, and cultural field within which the text was first produced, and to do so burdened by our own hard-to-identify but deeply determining cultural and social presuppositions.

For Gadamer, however, to see these factors as obstacles is to imagine that a text's meaning is itself essentially ahistorical, as if its being delivered over to the vicissitudes of cultural and historical change were a kind of semantic Fall, polluting an originally pristine and self-sufficient sense or significance. Gadamer's suggestion is that this is a fantasy; the meaning of any text is in fact essentially historical, because those who produce and receive it are essentially historical. The only kind of meaning that essentially finite, temporal human beings can construct and construe—the only kind of meaning there is for us—must share that finitude. No author can simply, purely create meaning; in saying something, she necessarily locates herself in a preexisting field of language and culture, and in relation to present and future audiences with preconceptions that are similarly historically specific. For no reader can be simply, purely receptive to the meaning of texts (or indeed, anything else) she encounters; in the absence of certain orienting assumptions, she would not even recognize that what she was encountering was a meaningful text, let alone what kind of text, and hence what kinds of questions might be addressed to that text.

Hence, it is confused to think that every interpretation's reliance upon presuppositions entails that all interpretations are necessarily biased or merely relative; this is what Gadamer castigates as the Enlightenment prejudice against prejudice. What matters is which presuppositions are relied upon in any particular interpretation, and how they bear the responsibility of making sense of the particular text. It is only in the process of pursuing the answers to some question or other that we might find that some specific presupposition of ours is in fact misapplied or in need of modification, or that some presupposition of the text must rather be regarded as a limiting or disabling aspect of its significance; this is how our encounter and exchange with the text allows us to differentiate good presuppositions from bad, enabling assumptions from mere prejudice. And it is precisely the historical distance between ourselves as readers and the text we read that allows us to deepen our understanding of it through just such a process of mutual exchange or dialogue—through what Gadamer calls our conversation with it.

But this conversation is not solely between the text and some given reader. It is also a conversation between past and present readers of that text (since part of what currently orients our reading of a text will be previous readings of it, and hence previous conversations between that text and its audiences), and a conversation (with both text and previous readers) about whatever the text is about—whatever phenomena or themes or concerns preoccupy it. Thus the conversation is many-cornered; hence the presuppositions of any given participant in it are both open to question by and capable of putting into question those of any other. In other words, we have the resources to distinguish in principle between better and worse interpretations of the text, and better and worse understandings of whatever the text is attempting to understand. And since the dialogical process through which we accomplish this is essentially historical, it is capable in principle of allowing for growth in understanding—in our understanding not only of the relevant text but of the broader culture of which it was a part, of developments in that culture since then (insofar as they bear upon our developing understanding of that text) and of the subject matter of the text (which is in part the subject matter of the ongoing cultural conversation about that text).

THE IDEA OF CONVERSATION: MISSING THE POINT

Gadamer's image of hermeneutic understanding as conversation thus develops the necessarily historical dimension of Rhees's notion of language as a conversation; it also reinforces his sense that what is at stake in the possibility of such discourse is the human capacity to make contact with, and grow in understanding of, reality—both the constituents of human reality, such as texts and cultures, and the extrahuman reality of which we are a part, and which our texts and cultures in large part struggle to confront. And various versions of this set of ideas are to be found in the postanalytic Anglo-American philosophical traditions.

They find a sophisticated, nuanced, and authentic role, for example, in the work of Alasdair MacIntyre, whose recounting of moral life in terms of practices and traditions presents both as the unfolding contexts of unending conversations about the meaning and significance of human actions and human forms of living.[3] For MacIntyre, a healthy and vital tradition does not—contrary to the views of his critics—demand that its inhabitants reinforce one another's views (any such demand would in fact indicate its impending demise as a field for genuine intellectual inquiry). It rather maintains a space within which they might fruitfully disagree; one might say, it keeps alive the possibility of surprise, and hence of genuine growth in one's understanding, without guaranteeing its advent.

However, other versions of these same ideas seem less aware of the damage that can be done if they are put to work in the wrong, or at least in incautious, ways; and the work of Oakeshott and Rorty seem to me to be exemplary in this respect. In the present context, I can only gesture toward the grounds for my suspicions of their conceptions of philosophy and the broader culture as essentially conversational;[4] but perhaps even the reader who wishes to contest my interpretations of their work can acknowledge that the positions I take them (erroneously) to occupy constitute genuine intellectual possibilities, and hence genuine dangers.

In my view, Michael Oakeshott's use of the notion of conversation in these kinds of context is essentially ambiguous in a way to which Rhees would have been particularly sensitive. Here, for example, is how he summarizes his view in "The Study of Politics in a University":

> A civilization (and especially ours) may be regarded as a conversation being carried on between a variety of human activities, each speaking with a voice, or in a language of its own; the activities (for example) represented in moral and practical endeavour, religious faith, philosophic reflection, artistic contemplation and historical or scientific inquiry and explanation. And I call the manifold which these different manners of thinking and speaking compose, a conversation, because the relations between them are not those of assertion and denial but the conversational relationships of acknowledgement and accommodation. (*Rationalism in Politics*, 187)

Much in this summary accords with Rhees's, Heidegger's, and Gadamer's position. In particular, it expresses a legitimate anxiety on Oakeshott's part that the conversation of culture not be dominated by one voice to the exclusion of all others (in particular the voice of scientific inquiry), or understood in the terms appropriate to that voice—as if the conversation as a whole were a single voice, a rational superinquiry into the Truth about Reality as such. But that anxiety often leads Oakeshott to characterize this conversation in different but equally general terms apparently drawn from (his conception of) another voice in the conversation, and which thereby succumb to, rather than over-come, the perennial temptation to confuse the whole with one of its parts.

For example, while rightly emphasizing the thought that conversation is an "unrehearsed intellectual adventure," hence lacking a single purpose or procedure that might determine its progress, he goes on to say, "[I]t is with conversation as it is with gambling, its significance lies neither in winning nor in losing, but in wagering" (*Rationalism*, 490). This idea of wagering may simply be meant to invoke the notion of risk or daring, of acting without denying the limits of one's capacity to control its out-come; but it also itself risks conjuring an image of mere play— of a conversation whose key tone is one of frivolity and super-ficiality, in which nothing real is at stake, and in which the significance of its outcome or conclusions is as nothing in com-parison with immersion in the process. It is as if, in order to avoid characterizing the conversation of culture in the terms appropriate to the scientific mode of inquiry, Oakeshott feels that he must avoid implying that its participants have any inter-est in deepening their understanding of that about which they converse, in confirming and enhancing their sense of contact with what is real (in themselves, their culture, and the world). And yet if, as Oakeshott himself rightly says, these participants must acknowledge one another, and if many of them understand their own activities as ways of achieving various forms of gen-uine understanding, how could they achieve such an acknowl-edgment without making the human concern for making con-tact with reality a central topic of their conversations?

In Richard Rorty's work, it is as if the ambivalence I see in Oakeshott's formulations—cited as a significant reference point for Rorty's own thinking—is resolved, but in favor of a sophis-tic interpretation of the idea of the conversation of mankind. At the end of *Philosophy and the Mirror of Nature*, Rorty asks what role is left for philosophy once it recognizes that its modern self-conception as a systematic account of the conditions for the possibility of knowledge, and hence as prior to any particular way of acquiring knowledge, is acknowledged to be the expression of a fantasy. He concludes that it must not take on any other systematizing ambitions, not even that of being systematically unsystematizing, but must rather aim to be unsystematically edifying.

> [Edifying philosophers] do not think that when we say something we must necessarily be expressing a view about a subject. We might just be *saying something*—participating in a conversation rather than contributing to an inquiry. Perhaps saying things is not always saying how things are. Perhaps saying *that* is not a case of saying how things are. [Edifying philosophers] suggest we see people as saying things, better or worse things, without seeing them as externalizing inner representations of reality. But this is only their entering wedge, for then we must cease to see ourselves as *seeing* this, without beginning to see ourselves as seeing something else. We must get the visual, and in particular the mirroring, metaphors out of our speech altogether. To do that we have to understand speech not only as not the externalizing of inner representations, but as not a representation at all. We have to drop the notion of correspondence for sentences as well as for thoughts, and see sentences as connected with other sentences rather than with the world. . . . Edifying philosophy aims at continuing a conversation rather than at discovering truth. (371–73)

Rorty's recoil from representational and correspondence models of knowledge may be genuinely edifying; but here it seems to drive him to an opposite and equally unedifying extreme. For he moves rather too swiftly from the thought that not all speech is a contribution to an inquiry, to the thought that all speech is nonrepresentational; and he moves equally swiftly from the thought that philosophical speech is not a representation of Reality as such, to the thought that philosophical speech is essentially opposed to saying how things are, to the discovery of truth, to making any form of contact with reality. And both fallacious chains of reasoning seem motivated by the belief that to talk of culture as a conversation, and of philosophy as a contributor to that conversation, is to divorce both from any interest in reality and in achieving an enhanced (or at least avoiding a degraded and damaging) understanding of the real. In so doing, however, they display a remarkably impoverished conception of the alternatives available to us in this domain.

There plainly are forms of conversation that have no real interest in engaging with reality—conversations where wit and entertainment, or just filling awkward silences, are the primary concern, and coming to a deeper understanding of anything is of no relevance whatever. And by no means are all such conversations essentially frivolous and superficial, lacking any worthwhile place in our lives. But to talk of some kinds of conversation as floating pleasurably or dully free of any concern with reality is to presuppose that other kinds of conversation are capable of making contact with what is real; such free-floating conversations are what they are only in the context of a life with language that is inherently open to the world, since there would otherwise be no possibility of a concern with reality from which we might sometimes, to our own benefit, turn away, and no meaningful words with which to do so in witty or effective ways. Hence to imagine all conversation as essentially opposed to any growth in understanding is in fact to imagine no conversation at all; it is to hollow out language altogether, leaving us with mere noises and marks spinning in a void. It is to obliterate the very possibility of discourse in Rhees's sense of that phrase.

If philosophers cannot find a space between metaphysical foundationalism on the one hand and talk of playing games with words on the other, then they will lose their grip on the sense of philosophy, and the sense of human life with language. At exactly the point at which we think that we have understood the meaning of things, we will be living an illusion. But nothing in the nature of the conversation of humankind can stop this from happening; even the idea that what we are participating in is best thought of as a conversation can itself be understood in such a way as to threaten the transformation of that conversation into what Heidegger would call idle talk (Emerson says rather that every word such people say chagrins us; Nietzsche speaks of nihilism). Perhaps one can, nevertheless, take comfort from the fact that for as long as there are philosophers whose contributions to the conversation take this kind of warning form, the sophist will not have the last word.

THREE

Lectures and Letters as Conversation

CAVELL AS EDUCATOR IN
Cities of Words

Stanley Cavell's recent publication *Cities of Words* (hereafter cited as *CW*), is a book that insists upon the fact that its origins lie outside itself. Its individual chapters all take the form of readings of the work of others—philosophers, psychoanalysts, filmmakers, novelists, and playwrights; each reading (with perhaps one exception) is of authors and texts that Cavell has discussed elsewhere in his published work, in some cases extensively; and its dedication (to the teaching fellows in Moral Reasoning 34) and introduction (subtitled "In the Place of the Classroom") confirm what the preface they flank begins by declaring: "The book of letters you have before you follows the course of a course of lectures called Moral Perfectionism, which I gave a number of times over the last decade and a half" (*CW,* ix).

Transcribing that written declaration, I am struck by the fact that the phrase "Moral Perfectionism" lacks the quotation marks that one would expect if it functioned simply as the name or title of the course of lectures concerned; in their absence, one can as well read this sentence as declaring that Moral Perfectionism, as Cavell understands it, *is* a course of lectures. In other words, Moral Perfectionism is not just one possible topic for a course of lectures on Moral Reasoning, but rather particularly calls out for expression in a course of lectures—as if lecturing, let's say establishing a certain kind of pedagogical relation between individuals, is internal to the responsibilities it asks its representatives to shoulder. And Cavell's readings of the members of the two film genres with which he pairs his other set of readings emphasize the need for and the possibility of education specifically through conversation—that of the woman by the man in what he calls comedies of remarriage, or that of the man by the woman in what he calls melodramas of the unknown woman. This comes out most explicitly in *It Happened One Night*, when Clark Gable subjects Claudette Colbert to a series of lectures on the proper way to do things, such as piggybacking or hitchhiking or doughnut dunking. As Cavell himself recalls in the preface to *Themes Out of School*, after one such outbreak, Gable declares, "Come to think of it, I ought to write a book about it"; to which his companion replies, "Thanks, Professor."

If there is such an internal relation between perfectionism, education, and conversation, then investigating the specific nature of this course of lectures might help us to understand what kind of conversational relation between teacher and student, and hence between any human pair whose common concern is the concern of moral perfectionism, is here in view. It might, in other words, allow us to see how the ideas of conversation and of (potentially radical) growth in understanding—already seen as made for one another in my earlier lectures—not only imply the idea of a certain pedagogical dimension to authentic human speech but also permit, even demand, expression in a pedagogical context.

But any such investigation will have to bear two things in mind: the nature of the original course of lectures, and the nature of the book that follows the course of that course. For a lecturer's relation to her audience necessarily differs from a writer's relation to her readers; and acknowledging that difference, or set of differences, must itself pose a pedagogical problem for any writer who aims to compose a written version of a set of lectures—that is, to present those lectures in the form of a book rather than to transcribe and publish a set of expanded lecture notes or to write a book on the same topic or textual material to which a set of lectures also refers. What kind of marriage or convergent transfiguration of these pedagogic genres might conceivably meet the conversational aspirations of the perfectionist? The subtitle of Cavell's book ("Pedagogical Letters on a Register of the Moral Life") suggests that the resultant genre is epistolary, but that simply generates a new question—namely, why should perfectionist pedagogical aspirations best be met by the transformation of lectures into letters?

Before I attempt to answer this question, a brief indication of what Cavell means by "moral perfectionism" might be of use to those unfamiliar with this aspect of his work but all too familiar with what Cavell himself would regard as perversions of perfectionism—variants of elitism which associate the idea of perfecting oneself with that of overlooking or violating the rightful claims of others upon us, and upon the social resources that we create and hold in common, and so appear to negate morality as such. Cavell's version of moral perfectionism certainly does cut across more familiar moral preoccupations with doing one's duty or maximizing the general happiness or cultivating one's virtues; and it also embodies an idea of the individual's truth to herself or to the humanity in herself. But it sees that self-concern as inseparable from a concern with society and the possibilities it holds out for others. For it understands the soul as on an upward or onward journey that begins when it finds itself lost to the world, and it requires a refusal of the present state of society in the name of some further, more cultivated or cultured, state of society as well as of the soul. This species of perfectionism further assumes that there is no final, as it were absolutely or perfectly cultivated, state of self and society to be achieved; rather, each given or attained state of self and society always projects or opens up another, unattained but attainable, state, to the realization of which we might commit ourselves, or alternatively whose attractions might be eclipsed by the attained world we already inhabit. In that sense, every attained state is (that is, can present itself as, and be inhabited as) perfect—in need of no further refinement; hence, the primary internal threat to this species of moral perfectionism is that of regarding genuine human individuality as a realizable state of perfection (even if a different one for each individual), rather than as a continuous process of self-perfecting (selfhood as self-improvement or self-overcoming). As Nietzsche might put it, such perfectionism is a matter of Becoming, not Being.

Cavell sees traces of this vision as pervading the Western tradition of moral thinking from its inception, and hence as forming a dimension of moral thinking as such rather than a family of specific moral theories. He has articulated its founding myth or primal story most clearly in terms adapted from its expression in Plato's *Republic*:

> Obvious candidate features are its ideas of a mode of conversation, between (older and younger) friends, one of whom is intellectually authoritative because his life is somehow exemplary or representative of a life the other(s) are attracted to, and in the attraction of which the self recognizes itself as enchained, fixated, and feels itself removed from reality, whereupon the self finds that it can turn (convert, revolutionize itself) and a process of education is undertaken, in part through a discussion of education, in which each self is drawn on a journey of ascent to a further state of that self, where the higher is determined not by natural talent but by seeking to know what you are made of and cultivating the thing you are meant to do; it is a transformation of the self which finds expression in the imagination of a transformation of society into something like an aristocracy where what is best for society is a model for and is modeled on what is best for the individual soul, a best arrived at in the view of a new reality, a realm beyond, the true world, that of the Good, sustainer of the good city, of Utopia. (*Conditions Handsome and Unhandsome*, 6–7)[1]

I hope that the connection between the general concerns of the earlier chapters and Cavell's idea of perfectionism as engendering growth in understanding through a distinctive mode of conversation is tolerably clear; and that my discussion of Heidegger's idea of the voice of conscience at least prepared the way for Cavell's perfectionist picture of the self as internally split or doubled, in a way that makes possible and is made possible by a certain kind of converse with oneself. But perhaps we already have enough preliminary guidance to begin seeking an answer to my question about lectures and letters as modes of conversation.

ORAL ORIGINS

The original course of Cavell's lectures was prepared for the Moral Reasoning section of Harvard's Core Curriculum, hence for large audiences of undergraduates in the arts and humanities for whom philosophy might not loom large in their academic programs or interests. Cavell tells us that he lectured twice a week for a semester: "The Tuesday lectures concerned central texts of moral philosophy, early and late . . . or literary texts presenting moral issues bearing on perfectionist preoccupations . . . , or philosophical presentations of texts by writers not usually considered by professional philosophers to be moral thinkers. . . . Thursdays were devoted to masterpieces (according to me) of American film from the so-called Golden Age of the Hollywood talkie" (*CW*, ix). The Tuesday texts included works by Aristotle, Kant, Mill, Nietzsche, Henry James, G. B. Shaw, and Shakespeare; the Thursday films included *The Philadelphia Story, Adam's Rib, Now, Voyager, Stella Dallas,* and *His Girl Friday.*

This bare summary suggests two central ways in which the philosophical texts, and the philosophical pertinence of certain nonphilosophical texts, with which Cavell proposes to concern himself are being made accessible to these students. First, since every film lectured on in the Thursday sessions was also screened for the members of the course, and since many of the nonphilosophical texts lectured on in the Tuesday sessions possess a real cultural fame, the course drew upon two ranges of experience with which course members who lacked any familiarity with the philosophical canon might be presumed to be equipped, and through which they might discover themselves to be already acquainted with the subject matter (according to Cavell) of the canonical philosophical texts. Second, the written record of the Tuesday sessions (although not those alone) demonstrates Cavell's mastery of the central and familiar, but nonetheless considerable, academic skills of clear expression, apt choice of illustrative example, and the provision of a penetrating, cumulative summary of the basic concepts and concerns of the author under consideration, in words of one's own that nevertheless maintain a fidelity to that author's own forms of expression, that anticipate and dissipate points of confusion or puzzlement without avoiding matters of genuine critical concern, and that convey something of the intrinsic interest and value of what is thereby laid out.

This, I take it, is what Cavell means when he talks of keeping "in the published chapters something of the sound of the original classroom lectures," "the sound of interesting, which means interested, academic lecturing" that he distinguishes from "the sound of a presentation to a scholarly organization, or a formal talk to a general public" and claims to love (*CW*, ix–x). If this is what one might mean by the provision of introductory lectures, then *Cities of Words* presents us with a set of introductory lectures to some of the most complex thinkers in Western philosophy—lectures whose value as introductions to their set texts would remain whatever one's final evaluation of the distinctive perfectionist dimension that concerns Cavell. And the point is worth dwelling on, since his (to me, incontrovertible) success in retaining that classroom sound in his prose demonstrates the reality of a register of Cavell's way with words that is not always evident in other genres of his writing, at least not with such even, sustained consistency as here, and so is persistently underestimated or entirely discounted. It is the sound of a born teacher, teaching.

But of course, to offer lectures on Hollywood movies, along with literary and psychoanalytic texts, as part of a course on Moral Reasoning whose initial reference point is the essays of

Emerson, under the aegis of one of the most eminent departments in the English-speaking philosophical world, is to offer a certain kind of provocation. For while its sheer existence suggests a certain commendable flexibility in the way in which that department is willing to conceive of morality, hence of moral philosophy and of philosophy as such, its content suggests a certain questionable limitation on that willingness, and hence a certain constraint in the philosophical world for which that department here stands proxy. For Cavell's claim is that the mode of moral encounter depicted and analyzed in these nonphilosophical texts is simply not registered in contemporary moral philosophy's division of its kingdom between Utilitarianism, Kantianism, and Virtue Theory, in part because those moral thinkers most sensitive to it (such as Emerson and Nietzsche) are not acknowledged as full-fledged philosophers; and yet, once that mode is highlighted, then even the writings of the founders of the three familiar schools of ethical theory can be seen to bear traces of its presence—more or less concealed or repressed acknowledgments of its reality and significance.

Furthermore, since this mode of moral encounter is, on Cavell's view, not merely depicted in nonphilosophical texts and contexts but analyzed, reflected upon, criticized, elaborated, reformulated—in short, reasoned about—then a further point of the mode of encounter his lecture course facilitates between philosophy and the arts is to invite an acknowledgment from philosophy that literature, cinema, and psychoanalysis have their own ways of responding to the claims of reason. Philosophy's sense of its place in the conversation of culture, and hence of its own distinctive nature, must confront that fact, on pain of failing to ask of itself what it asks of all other disciplines— reflection on its own conditions. And of course, the academic study of cinema, literature, and psychoanalysis has an obligation to confront the very same fact, or rather that face of it which declares the reality and significance of expressions of a recognizably philosophical impulse within their apparently distinct domains.

This is bound to unsettle our sense of whether, and if so how, philosophy is and can be professionalized—thus raising the question of philosophy's relation to, and proper place within, institutions of learning such as universities, those cities of words. In part, this is a function of the particular register of the moral life with which this book is concerned; for moral perfectionists characteristically diagnose those they address as inhabiting a state of moral disorientation or unintelligibility, and aim to attract them toward a recovery of themselves—thus achieving what Emerson calls self-reliance, or aversion from conformity. Is the taking of such an orientation to another a proper dimension of any philosophy lecturer's relation to his students? Can the authority of philosophy, let alone that of any pedagogical institution in which it participates, underwrite such a mode of encounter? Insofar as one thinks not, does this show the inadmissibility of any conception of philosophy that sees a perfectionist impulse as internal to it, or does it rather show that the survival of this dimension of moral philosophy—and so of philosophy—depends upon its refusal to settle for complete institutionalization?

From the perfectionist viewpoint, however, the kind of student body from which a Harvard University course on Moral Reasoning will recruit its members is a particularly apt audience for its purposes. For Cavell makes it clear throughout the book, although with particular emphasis and care in the chapter on Rawls, that the question posed by moral perfectionism is especially pertinent to those leading relatively privileged lives in their political community, and in ways which reveal that a perfectionist concern with the self is not only not necessarily, but is necessarily not, a purely selfish concern (one that turns us away from any concern with or for others). Against Rawls, Cavell argues that "there is no definitive defense, nor should there be in a democracy, against the sense of being compromised by the partiality, the imperfectness, of one's society's compliance with the principles of justice, when, that is, that partiality is one from which you gain relative advantage" (*CW*, 181). Even in a democracy whose basic arrangements come closest to the kind which all reasonable people would voluntarily accept (say, when choosing from behind a veil of ignorance), there will be some degree of existing injustice, and some extent to which certain citizens will be more materially advantaged than others. Hence, the relatively advantaged should feel that they are implicated in these arrangements, and exposed to the question of how far they can consent to a society with this degree of inequality in it. The perfectionist question is: how is one to live with this state of moral compromise? And the classroom in which Cavell raises and sharpens this question is full of relatively advantaged people, hence people who are being asked whether they have succumbed to the peculiar threat that democratic life raises for people in their kind of position—a guilty disdain and snobbery, "a tendency to distance oneself from the cultural costs of democracy, from the leveling down of taste, the mendacity of public discourse, the intolerance of indifference. The disdain may be understood as a reaction to blunt the guilt of advantage, a coarsening of political imagination that makes one indifferent to inequity and acquiescent in the state of nature that exists . . . wherever shared consent is not in effect" (*CW*, 189). Here, Cavell's perfectionist pedagogy has a political as well as a moral dimension; it conjoins the fate of philosophy with the fortunes of democracy, and it asks its audience to take seriously a kind of resentment of their own good fortune that is grounded in something other than specific failures of insufficiently just institutions—something more like a competent conviction that the existing moral ground of those institutions as such requires radical transformation.

A further, essential part of the process of transforming the lecture course into a book, Cavell tells us, was the opportunity to deliver the course at the University of Chicago, in the same twice-weekly format, but with twice as much time allotted to each lecture and with the course as a whole delivered over a full academic year. This allowed Cavell to get back into the spirit of the original course, but it also required that he commute from his Boston home to Chicago throughout that year.

> As I sat in Boston, more precisely in Brookline, one street from the Boston city limits, within earshot of Fenway Park, which mattered in October and would matter again in April and May, writing out documents of a certain intimacy to be delivered, a day or two after I completed them, to a shifting audience living a two-hour plane ride away, I came to think of these documents as a sequence of pedagogical letters, although I do not insist on referring to them that way in the book (since the idea of a chapter, as marking a segment of a life, is an equally apt and interesting concept). (*CW*, x)

This bracketed invocation of the idea of a chapter might seem to suggest that the image of these documents as letters is of limited importance—only one way of looking at them, perhaps merely the reflection of a purely autobiographical aspect of their composition. On the other hand, not all authors would invite their readers to attend to the etymological link between the internal divisions of a book and the internal segmentation of a life; and it is not usually part of anyone's idea of a chapter that it might equally aptly, equally interestingly, be conceived of as a letter. And since the subtitle of the book that was reborn in the classrooms of the University of Chicago in this particular way does insist on the idea of a letter (beyond the sense in which every use of words is a use of the letters that make them up, the basic population of any cities of words), I think we are licensed to look a little more closely at this self-description.

THE GENRE OF THE LETTER: WITHIN CAVELL'S WORK

The only other published work of Cavell's that explicitly assigns itself to this genre is his "A Cover Letter to Molière's *Misanthrope*," published in *Themes Out of School* (another title of some pedagogical interest). This was originally published as a way of justifying the inclusion of an essay on *Othello* in an issue of

Daedalus devoted to the topic of hypocrisy, and more specifically conceived of as a response to the narcissistic or misanthropic elements of Othello himself; a slightly modified version of that essay on *Othello* constitutes the closing pages of *The Claim of Reason*. What, from this complex nest of intertextuality, these traces of a self's unfolding converse with itself, might one draw for our purposes—from the perspective afforded by a sequence of pedagogical letters on perfectionism?

First, the character to whom the letter is addressed—Alceste—is someone who has withdrawn from the world of human society, which he disdains as full of show and artifice, insistently dissociating the public and the private, the outer and the inner. In other words, he judges that the world as it is is not acceptable, not wantable, and not because he is a victim of political injustice, either privately or as the member of a victimized class or race; and Cavell's first point in writing his letter is to acknowledge "that there may be room left, beyond private or public injustice, for refusing the world." From our point of view, I think it is clear that this is the room occupied by the women of the melodramas, hence by that side of the perfectionist temperament which refuses the world as it is, which finds itself unable to consent to its present arrangements as its own, as ones for which it is willing to speak, with which it is willing to go along, any further.

What Cavell suggests in his letter to Alceste is that this perfectionist refusal constitutes the philosophical significance of adolescence—that time in one's life when the public world as such, hence adulthood, is the thing we are asked to choose, to consent to. His further claim is that the continuing love of Alceste's friends for him from within that public world, despite their refusal to join him in his refusal—shown when at the end of Molière's play they go to seek him out—constitutes their recognition of the continuing significance of his refusal for them, and for their world. It shows that genuine adulthood can and should maintain an openness to adolescence, on pain of losing its sense of what is forgone should adolescence ever be altogether forgone—the sense that the public world is indeed open to judgment as a whole, beyond its specific failures of private and public justice, for failing to maintain its promise as a field of genuine possibilities for the individuals who inhabit it.

But of course, for Alceste's friends to feel the rebuke in his taking offense it is not necessary for them to join him in his self-exile; for the question of whether or not any given state of society merits such refusal can be settled only by each individual's determination, and hence is a matter over which individuals might reasonably differ. And by the same token, whether those who keep faith with their society do so hypocritically, or those who break faith with it do so fraudulently, must be a matter of individual judgment from case to case. The matter is not and cannot be settled simply by seeing whether an individual does or does not keep that faith—as if sincerity can only survive outside society, or fraudulence only within it. What will settle the matter for any competent judger is rather why and how any given individual keeps or breaks their faith—for example, whether in a way that acknowledges, or one that denies, the entitlement of others to differ in that judgment, and to regard this question of consent as always reopenable in the future.

In this context, Othello appears as someone whose sense of his own purity expresses a desire to dissociate himself from the vulnerabilities inherent in human nature; when he is confronted with their undeniable presence in himself by the one he loves, he ends by murdering her, and hence his hopes for himself. Call this the risk of narcissism in moral perfectionism. But unless one is prepared to run that risk, then we, and our polity, run the complementary risk of monstrous indifference—a willingness to go along with whatever tides of events, and degradations of political life, to which our polity might be subject, making of ourselves monsters of adaptability. On Cavell's perfectionist understanding of the matter, then, it is of vital democratic moment that we be prepared to credit revulsion and horror as conceivably political responses, as possible forms of conscience.

By bringing his letter back, in conclusion, to the specifically political matter of student protests against American policy in Vietnam, Cavell hints at the issue that his delivery of his later lectures on moral perfectionism makes more systematically explicit: the particular aptness of content to form in the context of an undergraduate audience. For then, the lecturer's articulation of adolescence as a moral and political phenomenon is addressed to adolescents; he thereby simultaneously acknowledges an aspect of his subject matter, an aspect of his audience, and an aspect of his own pedagogical situation.

Furthermore, Cavell's cover letter uncovers another text of his that he is retrospectively inclined to characterize (at least in part) as a letter; for he presents one strand or passage of a long early essay of his that he composed at the time of the student Vietnam protests as "a love letter to America."[2] In those passages, he compares the tragedy of *King Lear*, in which two fathers each produce the image of parents cannibalizing their children, to the effect of American foreign policy upon those in whose name it was prosecuted; he is therefore quite prepared to understand that to some to whom his love letter was addressed it might have seemed to be written out of hatred. In the later context of the cover letter, we can say that it amounts to his inhabitation of Alceste's position, or rather to his giving expression to the side of himself that sides with Alceste; although the fact that that earlier letter is addressed to those who do not share his revulsion entails that it also gives expression to the side of himself that sides against Alceste, and with his friends. In the even later context of the pedagogical letters, not only can we say that from this very early essay on, Cavell was always already giving expression to a perfectionist perspective; we can also say that he thinks of moral perfectionism as always already addressed not only to America but from it—as a form of political speech particularly prepared for and called for in the context of a political community founded on its identification with the human pursuit of happiness, and whose founding philosophical expression is to be found in the repressed voice of Emerson (and of course Thoreau).

Leaving aside the edification to be found in Cavell's own use of
the letter form elsewhere in his work, what might we learn from
a comparison between his present use of that form and its use by
other thinkers, particularly those included by Cavell within his
register of participants in the tradition (the ongoing conversation) of moral perfectionism? Cavell himself declares at the outset that "speaking of the segments as letters invokes an illustrious precursor in the line of moral perfectionism, Friedrich
Schiller's 'series of letters' *On the Aesthetic Education of Man*—
although Schiller's views of perfectibility and of the authority of
philosophy and, for that matter, the nature of morality and of
aesthetics are at variance with those advanced here" (*CW*, x).
Once again, this invocation might seem to amount to a simple
denial of relevance: if Schiller's conceptions of morality, aesthetics, philosophy, and perfectibility differ from Cavell's, and given
that his series of letters is not in fact the subject matter of any of
Cavell's book of letters, then what on earth might be left to give
point to his invocation as a partner in a conversation about letters as a medium for conversation?

One formal matter suggests a certain continuity within this
difference. For Schiller's final text emerges from a real epistolary situation: in 1793 Schiller wrote to his patron, the Duke of
Augustenburg, asking if he might first submit his ideas on the
philosophy of beauty in a series of letters to him before offering
them to the public, on the grounds that this freer form would
give his work more individuality and life, and his thoughts a
higher degree of interest.[3] In effect, then, the epistolary format
frees Schiller from any reliance upon what he calls in his first
letter more "scholastic modes" of expression; what he thereby
refuses to invoke is the authority of any particular philosophical
school, and hence any risk of sectarianism or borrowed weak-
ness, and indeed the authority of philosophy as such, insofar as

that is seen as dependent upon a certain kind of theory building, a certain kind of systematization of thought. His view is that the truth of any thought expressed in such scholastic form can and must be manifest—insofar as it is a truth—when it is given expression in nontechnical form, as a pronouncement of what Schiller calls "Common Reason"; and further, that when such truths are expressed in technical form, that which may highlight their claim upon our intellect "veils it again from our feeling."

> In order to lay hold of the fleeting phenomenon, [the philosopher] must first bind it in the fetters of rule, tear its fair body to pieces by reducing it to concepts, and preserve its living spirit in a sorry skeleton of words. Is it any wonder that natural feeling cannot find itself again in such an image, or that in the account of the analytical thinker truth should appear as paradox? (*AEM*, 1.4)

Cavell's pedagogical letters also aim to avoid such subjection to any philosophical school, although whereas Schiller's challenge is primarily to find ways of pursuing an essentially post-Kantian project while avoiding the pervasive reiteration of Kantian terminology, Cavell's essentially Emersonian project does not confront a parallel difficulty, since Emerson's understanding of his task is not to forge a distinctive technical terminology but rather to find ways of saying what he means to say by discovering or recovering a perfectionist register in language as such—in any and every one of the common words whose present conforming use so chagrins him. And this, of course, creates a different difficulty for Cavell; for it means that, where Schiller needs to find nontechnical ways of expressing a variety of Kantian thoughts but at least has a systematic body of Kantian thought upon which to draw in so doing, there is no comparable body of Emersonian thought for which nontechnical equivalents and extensions must be sought or might be found. Rather, Cavell must find his own specific range of expressions upon which to effect the same kind of operation that Emerson effects on specific ranges of terms in his various series of essays.

Cities of Words resolves this problem by broadening its range of reference beyond Emersonian essays in two particular ways: first, by finding a way of reading nonphilosophical texts (novels, plays, and particularly films) as expressions of something recognizable as Emersonian perfectionist ideals, and second by finding an Emersonian perfectionist register in an indefinite range of canonical texts in moral philosophy. This strategy not only frees Cavell from dependence upon the terminology of any particular philosophical author or school, even Emerson's (assuming that we grant him the status of "philosopher"), but also frees him from a dependence upon any distinctively philosophical terminology at all. More precisely: it allows him to demonstrate that the perfectionist dimension of philosophy is continuous with an inherent dimension of human modes of expression more generally—that perfectionism's concern is our relationship to the human means of expression as such, with our ability to conjoin inner with outer and private with public.

If one were to express this by saying that moral perfectionism concerns itself with the rights of human desire, then a further connection with Schiller's letters becomes evident. For as we saw, his avoidance of scholastic modes of expression was essentially designed to allow him to find words with which to reconnect truth with our feelings, to find a form in which intellectual truth can show itself to be genuinely, humanly attractive—say, desirable—in the absence of which, Schiller will go on to argue, it cannot be properly regarded as truth at all, but as a sorry skeleton of words from which the living spirit has departed.

Cavell's acknowledgment of an analogous goal emerges most explicitly in his reading of Mill, in which he connects the latter's famous grounding of the claims of utilitarianism in the fact that we find happiness desirable (in chapter 4 of *Utilitarianism*) with his rather less famous diagnosis of the present state of our desires (in chapter 3 of *On Liberty*).

> In our times, from the highest class of society down to the lowest, everyone lives as under the eye of a hostile and

dreaded censorship. Not only in what concerns others, but in what concerns only themselves, the individual or the family do not ask themselves, what do I prefer? Or, what would suit my character and disposition? Or, what would allow the best and highest in me to have fair play and enable it to grow and thrive? They ask themselves, what is suitable to my position? What is usually done by persons of my station and pecuniary circumstances? Or (worse still) what is usually done by persons of a station and circumstance superior to mine? I do not mean that they choose what is customary in preference to what suits their own inclination. It does not occur to them to have any inclination except for what is customary. Thus the mind itself is bowed to the yoke: even in what people do for pleasure, conformity is the first thing thought of; they like in crowds; they exercise choice only among things commonly done; peculiarity of taste, eccentricity of conduct are shunned equally with crime, until by dint of not following their own nature they have no nature to follow: their human capacities are withered and starved; they become incapable of any strong wishes or native pleasures, and are generally without either opinions or feelings of home growth, or properly their own. Now is this, or is it not, the desirable condition of human nature? (Mill qtd. in *CW*, 96–97)

If our present condition is such that we have no feeling, preferences, desires of our own (what, as we saw earlier, Cavell elsewhere calls "amentia"), then it is one in which we do not ask of ourselves: is this condition of ours, of mine, desirable? Given Mill's conception of us as fundamentally desiring creatures, this condition amounts to one in which we do not realize or actualize our own nature, and he writes so as to awaken us to the question of the desirability of our state, and hence to show us that we have a right to our own desires, and in particular a right to have them recognized as touchstones for social criticism and reform. This is the Millian mode of expressing Cavell's variant on

Schiller's perception that a touchstone of truth is its attractiveness, its capacity to address and awake our desire, the ability of our feelings to find themselves in its expression.

It is part of Schiller's conception of aesthetics that the authentic expression of desire is a realization of what he calls the play-drive, which is a synthesis of—at once the result of a reciprocal action of, and the condition for the full realization of—two other drives: the sense-drive (which impels the individual to realize every aspect of himself in the realm of matter) and the formal drive (which impels him freely to harmonize the diversity of his actual manifestations). Schiller thinks of the play-drive as reconciling change with identity, becoming with absolute being; it is the achievement of genuine human individuality, that conjunction of being and becoming that is the identity of the person through time. The overlap with Emerson's conception of the self as doubled or split between its present or attained state and its unattained but attainable state is not far to seek.

But my concern is to emphasize the connection between form and content in Schiller's work at this critical point. For given his claim that a touchstone of his account's truth must be its ability to elicit our desire, call this its aesthetic achievement, that achievement must itself be a manifestation of the play-drive. And the most obvious way in which his series of letters might be understood as a manifestation of that drive is surely the way they play with words—what two of his translators have called a "dance with concepts," in which the controlled but endlessly shifting pairings, oppositions, and relations of subordination and coordination between terms reflect what he sees as the interstrife and interplay of the elements of the psyche for which they stand. An essential part of this process is that Schiller finds that his key terms can be used authentically or inauthentically— in such a way as to identify a psychic phenomenon with one of its possible forms or states, usually the inauthentic one, or so as to reveal the essential difference between what that phenomenon usually is and what it might be if properly cultivated.

In other words, part of what is involved in coming to understand and to achieve aesthetic education, call it human cultivation or a genuinely lettered (a literate, cultured, and conversable) state, is cultivating the ability to mean words otherwise—to find contexts and modes of employment that reveal the limitations of common use and the possibility of uncommon but revealing alternatives, and the internal relation between those two possibilities (the necessity of a term's having both possible modes of use for it to be an expression of the relevant concept). The appearance of paradox in Schiller's prose is thus inevitable, as he warns us in his first letter; but the reality of the situation is that his words would otherwise be a mere sorry skeleton, binding the essentially transformative phenomena they register in fetters of rules. And without wishing to deny the differences between Schiller's ways of exploiting the play of words and Emerson's (hence Cavell's) aversive uses of them, it would be equally misleading to deny the continuities.

St. Paul

Another generic model for letter writing glancingly mentioned in *Cities of Words*, but not assigned to the tradition of moral perfectionism, is that of the Christian Epistles. These, too, are documents of a certain intimacy, composed by individuals charged with a certain spiritual responsibility, at a certain distance from the collective audience to which they are addressed, and concerning the conditions of that community's existence—hence essentially political in nature. In terms of the four genres of the New Testament, these Epistles fall between Acts and Apocalypse: they extend or exemplify the community-founding work inspired by the Gospels (one of which Cavell includes within the perfectionist tradition) and recorded in the Acts of the Apostles; and their edificatory guidance is offered in the light of a shared sense of the world's impending, absolute end. Accordingly, the transfiguration of individual and communal existence that they aim to secure has a commensurably apocalyptic register. And it is this aspect of the Epistles from which Cavell takes care to dissociate his moral perfectionism (which means also to associate it) in his letter on Ibsen, and Ibsen's association of marriage with a mode of change that is both miraculous and redemptive in *A Doll's House:*

> There is a change associated with salvation in the Christian Bible, First Corinthians 15 (a portion of which Emerson quotes in "Self-Reliance"): "Behold! I show you a mystery. We shall not all sleep, but we shall all be changed, in a moment, in the twinkling of an eye, at the past trumpet. For the trumpet shall sound, and the dead shall be raised incorruptible, and we shall be changed. For the corruptible must put on incorruption and the mortal must put on immortality." Linking this to the change called marriage puts marriage (whatever that will be recognized to be) under mortal, or say religious, pressure in the modern world, namely to achieve incorruptible union in a world none of whose corruptible institutions can validate the fact of genuine marriage, not church or state or family or gender or allowed sexuality. The uncanniness of the fit between Paul's Letter . . . and the end of Ibsen's *A Doll's House* is unlaughably comic, or dreamlike, when you consider that the twinkling of an eye in which Nora's change comes about occurs at bedtime, when, as Torvald abruptly discovers, she is not, and he is, preparing to go to bed ("We shall not all sleep"). . . .
>
> Some extreme statement is being suggested here about the secularization of modern life, about the relocating or transforming of what is important or interesting to human life, as if turning our attention from celestial to terrestrial things, or rather suggesting that their laws are not different. (*CW,* 261–62)

This passage suggests a certain mysteriousness in the relation between Paul and Ibsen here, hence between religious and secular forms of perfectionism: is the idea of change as radical transfiguration relocated or rather transformed in its secularization? If the idea of turning our attention from heavenly to earthly things is better put as a suggestion that their laws are not different, relocation would seem the better model. And of course, once the Christian communities relinquished their expectation of imminent actual apocalypse, they too began the work of relocating the idea of incorruptible union in the here and now, the everyday—coming to understand it as that of a community endlessly striving to realize individual dying to the self, with the corruptible flesh opposed to the incorruptible Spirit of an inherently, creatively self-abnegating God (not the body opposed to the soul).

The unlaughably comic or dreamlike fit between Paul and Ibsen in this respect is in fact already evident in Paul's Epistle alone, as when—for example—its rhetoric of the mortal putting on immortality ("O death, where is thy sting?") is immediately juxtaposed with a chapter of detailed instruction about such mundane matters as the timing of collections, admonitions about the virtues and vices of particular individuals and households, and warnings about the author's future travel plans. And a certain dreamlike awareness of the internal relation between the content of these letters and their form—in particular the way that form at once mirrors and foresees their recipients' aspirations for change—is evident in, for example, the third chapter of Paul's Second Epistle to the Corinthians:

> Do we begin again to commend ourselves? Or need we, as some others, epistles of commendation to you, or letters of commendation from you? Ye are our epistle written in our hearts, known and read of all men: Forasmuch as ye are manifestly declared to be the epistle of Christ ministered by us, written not with ink, but with the spirit of the living God; not in tablets of stone, but in fleshy tables of the heart. . . . Not that we are sufficient of ourselves to think anything as of ourselves; but our sufficiency is of God; who also hath made us able ministers of the new testament; not of the letter, but of the spirit, for the letter killeth, but the spirit giveth life.

We read here of a spiritual imperative that will reunite the spirit and the letter, the public assertion of law and its inner inscription, so that the community of those to whom this epistle is addressed will each become that epistle, a creaturely embodiment of its meaning, which means a realization of the self-abnegation that its composers exemplify when they say that they exist as authors of their epistles only insofar as God exists in them. Hence, to become a Christian is to strive to become an epistle of Christ—a life-giving letter, a site in which the transfiguration of corruptible into incorruptible flesh is unending, and constitutes an address to all who have eyes to see, and ears to hear.

There is no denying the extremity of this vision, or of the process of its realization or domestication. The question is: is the transfiguration envisaged by such secular perfectionists as Ibsen and Emerson (and Cavell) any less radical or dreamlike? Cavell suggests a fundamental difference in the introduction to his book of letters, when explaining why he does not take up perfectionisms based on a religious perspective in the pages to come:

> The sense of disappointment with the world as a place in which to seek the satisfaction of human desire is not the same as a sense of the world as cursed, perhaps at best to be endured, perhaps as a kind of punishment for being human. (*CW*, 3)

Cavell objects here to any idea of the world as unchangeably disappointing, and hence not something we can respond to by feeling called upon to change it, either individually or collectively. But not all religious ideas of the world as disappointing deny the malleability of this aspect of it; what they do deny is the possibility of changing it in the absence of divine aid—call it grace, a central topic of Paul's Epistles. And they conjoin this reference to the extrahuman or celestial with a conviction that it has already made itself available to us, and that one fully human being has revealed what it would be like to remake ourselves and our world in its image. Put otherwise, the Incarnation at once reveals us to be originally sinful and offers us redemption from it. The difficulty is to see how the Christian form of life simultaneously realizes both aspects of this conception. But is that really any more of a mystery than Ibsen's idea of marriage as an incorruptible union?

Plato

Another philosophical epistolary model that goes unmentioned in *Cities of Words*, but seems nonetheless pertinent given the centrality of Plato to Cavell's sense of the moral and cultural origins of moral perfectionism, is the sequence of thirteen letters reportedly first included in Thrasyllus's edition of Plato's works.[4] Many doubt their authenticity: we have no record of their existence before the end of the third century BC, one hundred and fifty years after their putative composition, and we know that many such "letters" of famous personages originated as exercises in schools of rhetoric, and others were "forged" for various reasons. On the other hand, the more specific reasons for doubting that Plato was their author seem to turn primarily upon their content, and the judgment that it simply does not accord with what we know the real Plato's real views to be; and this means that these doubts can be subverted insofar as we can subvert that judgment. In short, the question of their authenticity and the question of who Plato is (philosophically speaking) are inseparable; everything turns on how we read him, and hence on how we read them.

From the point of view of our particular interests, then, Plato's letters form an interesting counterpoint to Cavell's cover letter to Alceste: the latter has a real author and a fictional addressee, the former has a real addressee and a (possibly) fictional author. But our primary concern is their content, and most specifically the content of the letter generally judged to be least unlikely to have come from Plato's pen—the seventh. For it famously contains a "digression" (342–44c) on knowledge, language, and philosophy in which Plato expresses skepticism about the possibility of giving expression to his philosophical insights in the form of a scholarly treatise. Recalling from earlier dialogues his particular reasons for doubting that names and definitions can assure our grasp of the Forms to which they supposedly correspond, he concludes,

> Only when all of these things—names, definitions, and visual and other perceptions—have been rubbed against one another and tested, pupil and teacher asking and answering questions in good will and without envy—only then, when reason and knowledge are at the very extremity of human effort, can they illuminate the nature of any object.
>
> For this reason, anyone who is seriously studying high matters will be the last to write about them and thus expose his thought to the envy and criticism of men. What I have said comes, in short, to this: whenever we see a book, whether the laws of a legislator or a composition on any other subject, we can be sure that if the author is really serious, this book does not contain his best thoughts; they are stored away with the fairest of his possessions. And if he has committed these serious thoughts to writing, it is because men, not the gods, "have taken his wits away." (7.344b–c)

One might see here a general condemnation of writing as a vehicle for philosophical insight, except for two key points: first, a little earlier our author declares that "if these matters are to be expounded at all in books *or lectures*, they would best come from me" (7.341d, my emphasis), which suggests that the difficulty applies to speech as well as writing, and also that it is not insuperable; and second, the stronger, unqualified condemnation of writing just quoted is itself advanced in writing—more specifically, it inhabits the intimate distance established through a sequence of correspondence between a particular teacher and a particular individual or group of individuals.

Perhaps, then, when Plato says that "this knowledge is not something that can be put into words like other sciences," his condemnation is not of words but of their being used in philosophy as they are used in other sciences—in the form of books or other compositions that lay down the law, that give no room for teacher and pupil to test and rub up against one another the various ideas to which they are giving expression. For that extended, intensive process of friction can alone produce what Plato declares is the goal of his teaching: "after long-continued intercourse between teacher and pupil, in joint pursuit of the subject, suddenly, like light flashing forth when a fire is kindled, it [this knowledge] is born in the soul and straightway nourishes itself" (7.341c).

The compositional challenge philosophy sets, then, is to find oral and written ways that facilitate this kind of illuminating intercourse, a conversational exchange that can find one kind of fulfillment in face-to-face dialogues in the agora, another in courses of lectures in the schools, and perhaps another in epistolary correspondence. Then a book of letters such as *Cities of Words* might be seen as a way of continuing a mode of dialogical lecturing, of engendering the requisite discursive space in book form both by setting up and discovering correspondences of thought and expression between the individual thinkers and artists that it puts into dialogue across and within chapters, and by allowing individual readers the freedom to rub the formulations of each chapter against those of others and against her own, to create her own pairings of chapters, and repeatedly to revisit earlier contributions to the conversation, in the light of any of its later participants.

Cavell alludes to this freedom when explaining his sense that he asks his readers to read fast as well as slowly:

> [This idea] warns not only that you must leave a work prematurely but that there is no given order that we know is the best one in which to read what you are drawn to read. . . . There are many ways of sequencing the written texts and sequencing the films, as well as of choosing the pairings between films and texts, that appear in the coming chapters. Each way would yield its own accents. . . . If the idea of

reading the assigned films as instances manifesting a dimension of moral thinking traceable throughout Western culture is sound, then any pairing of one of these films with one of the assigned books should produce interesting, surprising results. (*CW*, 15)

I take it that this business of pairing and re-pairing is meant to apply not only to the texts that form the subject matter of each letter but also to the letters themselves, and such operations are of course far easier to effect as a reader than as a member of a lecture course. But in the vicinity of Plato's invocation of conversational discourse, and remembering that Cavell finds the chronological origin of moral perfectionism in Plato's Myth of the Cave, as he finds the essence of his two film genres to lie in their participation in (a pair of) stories or myths, with each contributing to the myth's development by proposing new clauses or provisions to the founding myth, we might further say that the "Tuesday" letters of *Cities of Words* propose their texts as clauses in the telling and retelling of a philosophical myth, or contributions to a conversation whose origins are essentially mythical, and for whose present health and fecundity—as a myth by which we make sense of ourselves and our lives—we are being invited to take responsibility. We might think of this suggestion as proposing a pairing of certain passages on myth from *The Claim of Reason* and *Pursuits of Happiness*.[5]

If, however, we understand Plato's purpose in his correspondence to be that of testing out the philosophical viability of letter writing, then it is important to place this passage of the seventh letter in its epistolary context; in so doing, two features of this context become salient for us. First, this so-called digression in the seventh letter is in fact motivated by a particular concern: the question of philosophy's relation to language is raised by Plato's need to determine whether or not Dionysius, the ruler of Syracuse, is a tyrant or a (budding) philosopher-king. And for Plato, this turns on two things: first, whether or not Dionysius wrote a book on philosophical first principles, and second, whether he took responsibility for a particular letter he had written (concerning the well-being of Plato's friend and representative Dion). In other words, Dionysius's claim to be a genuine student of Plato would have been betrayed as much by his failure to make his life correspond to his letters (thus making those letters his own, owning them as his) as it would by his composing the wrong kind of book.

And this question about Dionysius links in turn to the broader concerns of the whole sequence of Plato's letters—for they are addressed to various individuals in Syracuse and concern the failure of Plato's most extended attempt to give political realization to his philosophical ideals. The attempt, of course, famously ended in failure; and the letters offer a variety of reasons for it. Central among them is what Plato portrays as Dionysius's failure to treat with respect Plato's closest ally on Syracuse, Dionysius's brother by marriage, Dion. In other words, the political failure of this philosophical project is seen as pivoting around Dionysius's failure to treat Plato's friend (and hence Plato) as a friend (which may be why Plato's seventh letter conjoins Dionysius's philosophical failures with his failures of friendship—as if, since his studies had not found this kind of expression in his life, his life condemned his claim to be a genuine student of philosophy). This gives some support to Cavell's reading of Aristotle in *Cities of Words*, a reading which argues not only that the bonds of any true political community are bonds of friendship but that the study of friendship—that is, true discursive conversation about friendship—is internal at once to genuine friendship and to genuine philosophical understanding.

It may also be worth noting that Plato's letters as a whole take on a particular coloring—one of intimate, detailed, and forceful rebuke. True, this tone is rather too persistently pervaded by a spirit of polemical self-defense, or rather self-exculpation, for the reader's comfort—as if the author of these letters is rather too much concerned to make clear the purity of his own conscience, and rather too little concerned with the political and philosophical implications of his failure. But they are clearly an instance of what Cavell, in *Cities of Words*, calls passionate speech, in which an individual takes a stand in relation to other specific individuals that is not authorized by convention or rule but rather makes a claim on those he addresses—a claim to have the right to address an intimate rebuke to them; and to make that claim is necessarily to expose oneself to the risk of rejection, or at least to an equally intimate rebuke. In this way, Plato's letters exemplify Cavell's uninsistent acknowledgment of the connection between moral perfectionism, politics, and the singling out of individuals by individuals, on ground no more secure than each individual's sense of what they are willing to give to, and to take from, the other—which forms of rebuke and praise might constitute a way of furthering their relationship and which might constitute its ending.

Heidegger

The idea of a philosopher's Syracuse, and of a certain tonal failure in its acknowledgment (amounting to its denial), naturally lead us to another point of reference for Cavell's book of letters, this one glancingly mentioned in his letter on *Mr. Deeds Goes to Town*—Martin Heidegger's 1951 lectures entitled *Was Heisst Denken?*[6] But the transition is, to say the least, overdetermined: for Heidegger originally delivered his lectures at a highly charged transitional moment in his career. They were the first he had been permitted to give at Freiburg since he had been forbidden to teach by the French occupying powers, and the last he would deliver before his formal retirement from the university. Hence, it is not surprising that one of their central concerns is with what it is to be a teacher and thinker, what it might be to betray that calling, and how that calling fits—or rather fails to fit—with the pedagogical institution of the university.

As with Plato's turn from writing in writing, so Heidegger's turning away from the university as a site for teaching and thinking takes place on that very site, and so amounts to a certain kind of turning toward it—an implicit claim that that refusal of the present claims of the university is how he takes up his responsibilities as a teacher and thinker within its precincts. The perfectionist implication—surely mirrored in Cavell's aversive reconstruction of the syllabus and format of his university's standing conception of moral reasoning—is that true teaching and thinking are at once a turning toward and a turning away from prevailing conceptions of teaching and thinking, that the calling of the teacher calls for the enactment of a transition from what teaching and thinking are to what they might become.

Further points of contact with Cavell's way of marking his transition from the site of the university are not hard to find. First, the words of Heidegger's book *What Is Called Thinking?* confront their readers from the outset with the distinction between oral and written modes of the human voice. For those words are presented as transcriptions of lectures—and thus at once as mere representations of the original oral performance, and yet also as the indispensable supplement or fulfillment of that performance (for if Heidegger had truly thought of the work of the original lectures as essentially dependent on their oral delivery, he could have had no thought of publishing written versions of them). The implication is that the work of those lectures depends upon composing words in such a way as to retain the marks of speech, but speech that essentially looks forward to its remarking in writing.

The form of that writing is not, of course, epistolary; but it is nonetheless strikingly relevant to Cavell's parallel formal problem. For Heidegger's book is divided into lectures that are divided from each other by passages entitled "Summary and Transition." Their apparent purpose is to allow the lecturer to go over the key points of the preceding presentation and prepare the ground for the next, as if acknowledging the difficulty of attaining a perspicuous surview of a course of thought addressed to the ear rather than the eye. But then their retention in this transcription of the lectures would have no point. If, however, struck by this trace of their original mode of delivery, we return to their content, we find that it exceeds their advertised function; in them, Heidegger is as likely to take steps that are nowhere else taken, and that are as essential to his progress, as in the lectures "proper." That is, the lectures could as easily be read as transitional between the passages of "summary and transition"; more precisely, each portion of the text is essentially transitional, because the text as a whole is essentially transitional. It enacts Heidegger's Nietzschean (one might say, perfectionist) picture of the genuine thinker and teacher—like the genuine human being—as essentially in transition: as Heidegger transcribes Zarathustra's thought, "Man, unless he stops with the type of man as he is, is a passage, a transition; he is a bridge; he is 'a rope strung between the animal and the superman'" (*What Is Called Thinking?* 60).

Applied to the thinker and teacher himself, then, progress on the way of thought must be transitional, a passage from one's present self-understanding to an unattained but attainable self-understanding; hence it is a matter of reading oneself, of deriving guidance for the future from one's best past self-understanding. This, one might say, requires the ability to achieve a certain kind of intimate distance from oneself, treating one's own thoughts as one would the thoughts of another—as if they can best bear fruit for the future if one takes them as an expression of an aspect of oneself from which one has already departed or become distant.

I hear these ideas at play in the opening paragraph of Cavell's preface to *Cities of Words*, when he says:

> The book differs from the lectures most notably in the circumstance that the secrets of its ending and the mysteries of its beginning are here fixed, for you and for me. It is the same man saying "I" here as said "I" there, but the you, whom I address here, unlike the students and friends in the classroom, are free to walk away from any sentence or paragraph of it without embarrassment to either of us, and indeed to drop the course at any time without any penalty other than its own loss. (ix)

It is not only books and courses of lectures whose endings are secret and whose beginnings are mysterious; the same can be said of individual human lives, hence of the individual for whom the delivery of the lectures and the publication of the book were and are events in his life. In declaring their difference from one another, that man also declares their identity: since they have the same author, the differences they declare are internal to his sense of himself. Moreover, that same declaration shows him to be moving on from them, not only from the institutional context that might permit their oral redelivery but also from their written transfiguration. The authorial "I" is, and is no longer, here with us, his readers; while every word remains one he has composed and uttered, and hence his own, his to own, behind which he stands, he has also always already walked away from every sentence and paragraph of the book they make up, long before any of us choose to do so. Cavell's prefatory words thereby declare that human individuals are always constituted by this mortal, Schillerian play of identity-in-difference, hence always open to the perfectionist address to this internal duplicity or doubledness, this awareness that what we at present are is not all there is to us, not all that we might, and are free to, become.

How, then, might one declare this internal perfectionist self-differentiation—how enact in writing this capacity to maintain an intimate distance from oneself? Heidegger achieves this by subjecting his earlier thought to an implicit but radical critique in his lectures—by, for example, rethinking the significance of the human hand, in ways that exceed but are prepared for by his use of the word and its cognates in *Being and Time*—as well as by treating his initial, guiding thought in the lectures themselves ("Most provoking in our thought-provoking time is that we are still not thinking") as if it were the utterance of another. And he invites his readers to take the same attitude to his transcribed lectures—to see them as a point of departure for their own thinking, expressive of a mode of understanding that they can grasp only by going on from, hence going beyond, them.

Cavell, I want to suggest, achieves the same general goal by composing letters. On the one hand, they are letters to us, epistles transmitting his present best understanding of the thinkers that are their subject matter, and inviting us to respond to that understanding of them, by way of qualification, elaboration, or reasoned rejection. But they can also be seen as letters to the thinkers that they discuss, hence as implicitly inviting us to think of those thinkers' original texts as akin to letters—documents of a certain intimacy composed for individuals imagined as being at a certain distance from their author (in time and space), texts meant as a contribution to a Gadamerian conversation. And the further fact that these letters are responses to authors upon whom Cavell has not only lectured a number of times but has written about in other forums suggests that we might think of them as Cavell's letters to himself—epistolary responses to his earlier self, further articulations of a conversation with himself in which he is always already engaged insofar as he is genuinely teaching and thinking.

<hr>

In short, Cavell pictures himself to us, and so invites us to picture ourselves, rather as Paul depicts himself and his addressees in his letters—not so much as beings who write and receive pedagogical epistles, but as essentially epistolary beings, living epistles for ourselves and for others (or as beings who can fail so to live). In this sense, human beings cannot but exist in the place of the classroom (as Cavell's introduction styles it); to be is to be-in-the-classroom. To lose any interest in that conversational place would thus be to lose an interest in one's life as one's own; to drop the course that teaches us this would mean dropping any conception of our lives as capable of following a course, as under pedagogical guidance, if not our own then some repressed or anonymous other. Some penalty.

Redeeming Words

In the previous chapter, I noted in passing that Heidegger's *What Is Called Thinking?* is glancingly invoked just once in *Cities of Words*, as underwriting the perception (attributed to *Mr. Deeds Goes to Town*) that the desire to think is internal to the possibility of thinking. I did not there remark (as Cavell has noted repeatedly elsewhere) that in the same text Heidegger associates thinking with thanking. Putting those two associations together now, we might discover the thought that thinking is an expression of the desire to give thanks, hence an expression of gratitude. But for what? Above all, perhaps, for the capacity to think; but surely also for the continued existence of a world capable of eliciting our desire to think—a world in which we can take that kind of interest, one which repays that interest, hence a world of things to appreciate or appraise. And if thinking is a form of appraisal that is also an expression of gratitude, then philosophy (or whatever, for Heidegger, inherits that cultural task) must be a mode of giving praise.[1]

One can certainly think of Cavell's epistolary book as a series of letters in praise of great men and women—an expression of gratitude for their existence (on screen, on stage, and behind the page) that takes the form of a (sometimes radical) reappraisal of the interest they have for him, and that he invites us to share, so that both his and our interest in them might be reoriented or recalibrated, and thereby (let us say) appreciate. And of course, as such an expression, they exemplify a structural feature of moral perfectionism, with its requirement that one acknowledge particular others as exemplary of the mode of self-reliance or self-differentiation to which one aspires—in short, as befriending one's unattained self.

The task of giving praise as such has been under suspicion by philosophy since its beginnings in Plato, who makes clear his suspicions of the authority claimed by the Athenian genres of eulogy and encomium (with their subordination to matters of self-interest and political advancement rather than truthful representation), and presents a portrait of Socrates as someone whose eulogies are ironized and who is unwilling to sit still for eulogies from others—and yet who is undeniably deserving of discriminating appreciation, and is unusually well-placed to exercise it.[2] But what is more immediately under suspicion in the cases we have analyzed is the worthiness of Cavell's chosen objects of praise—most obviously, the merits of the movies he conjoins with canonical figures in literature and philosophy, but also the merits of figures only controversially to be called philosophers (not to mention his controversial sense of where the true merits of the work of the canonical philosophers is to be found). And this suspicion is hard to disentangle from a suspicion about the worthiness of the giver of such praise—perhaps a suspicion about his competence in nonphilosophical fields, perhaps a suspicion of his sincerity. Can he really be serious in taking (and asking us to take) this kind of interest in these human beings and their undeniably idiosyncratic works?

It might be thought that the difficulty in finding the proper measures for such praise—measures, that is, at once for the worthiness of the object and the worthiness of its giver—can hardly be internal to philosophy as such, but rather at best to philosophy's perhaps misguided ventures into aesthetic or moral terrain. But this thought (which unquestioningly locates aesthetics and ethics as distinct topics within the philosophical domain rather than as ineliminable dimensions of the philosophical enterprise whatever its putative subject matter) underestimates the difficulty, in at least two respects. First, it fails to appreciate that there can be no philosophy without a preliminary sense (however provisional) of what counts as doing philosophy, and no such orientation without the (however implicit) identification of examples of doing philosophy, hence without the choice of exemplary texts and exemplary philosophers—call it the acknowledgment of a canon. And any such appreciation of the work of others itself asks for appraisal. Second, if one's choice of philosophical exemplars includes that of Heidegger and Wittgenstein, then one inherits a further reason for finding the burdens and trials of praise in philosophy to be ubiquitous.

For the Heidegger of *Being and Time*, all forms of human understanding are informed by moods or (more generally) modes of attunement; to grasp entities as the kinds of entities they are is to grasp their meaning or significance—not only as having a particular nature and as handy for practical or theoretical engagement (in terms of the basic articulations of a discursive cultural field) but also as mattering to us, as having a value or worth that is ultimately to be traced to the necessities and agreements constitutive of human interests and purposes. In short, the world's availability to us is a function of fundamentally evaluative comprehension—it is a species of appraisal or appreciation; and since philosophical understanding is one more form of human understanding, the same must be true of it. In short, phenomenological discourse at once retraces and manifests the attunements internal to our cognitive grasp of the world; even for the early Heidegger, then, if not quite in his later words, thinking is thanking.

For Wittgenstein, as Cavell emphasizes most forcefully in *The Claim of Reason*, all philosophical investigations are grammatical—they take the form of reminders about the kinds of things we say about phenomena; and he claims not only that "grammar tells what kind of object anything is" (*PI*, 372)—hence that it gives expression to the essence of things—but also that our concepts (and hence their grammar) "are the expression of our interest" (*PI*, 570). In other words, the criteria in terms of which objects count for us (as objects of a specific kind) also make manifest which distinctions and differences matter to us; hence to grasp the grammar of a word is at once to grasp how and why we discriminate. Here is one sense in which one might claim that judgments of fact and judgments of value hang together—more precisely, that agreement in judgments, as manifest in our criterial attunements, is an agreement in valuing.

It would seem to follow that even the communication of a fact is dependent upon an agreement in evaluation, rather than the other way around. And Cavell's reading of Wittgenstein consequently suggests that what can comprehensibly be said is what is found to be worth saying. When it is not, we have the phenomenon cited in chapter 2, and reencountered in chapter 3, under the heading of amentia: "[T]he degree to which you talk of things, and talk in ways, that hold no interest for you, or listen to what you cannot imagine the talker's caring about . . . is the degree to which you consign yourself to nonsensicality, stupify yourself" (*Claim of Reason*, 95). This is a phenomenon of human life with speech as such, hence as evident outside philosophy as it is within; but it is just as capable of evincing itself within philosophy, and to conceive of philosophy as Wittgenstein does is to assign the philosopher the task of resisting it wherever it manifests itself. For to remind us of the grammar of our words just is to remind us that, and how, we appraise the world—it is to recall us to our vocation as appreciators of reality and of our fellow appreciators of reality; it invites us to take responsibility for—to be responsive to—the true worth of our interlocutors, their locutions, and the objects of those locutions. And such a responsibility makes the question of worth and its measures, hence the question of praiseworthiness, undismissable.

Wittgenstein once remarked that he would have liked to say about his work what Bach wrote on the title page of his *Orgelbüchlein:* "To the glory of the Most High God, and that my neighbour may be benefited thereby."[3] To say such a thing about one's work would be to identify it as a form of praise, and (certainly for Wittgenstein) so to identify it would itself be to praise it—it would exemplify self-appraisal as praise. Does the fact that he does not in the end actually say this about his work show that he is ultimately denying this desire of his, and thus declaring that he felt his work did not deserve such a self-appraisal? Or is his decision to specify the desire in making manifest his reluctance to satisfy it in fact a way of acknowledging it, hence a way of declaring his persisting sense of a kinship between grammatical appraisal and the religious believer's way of giving praise to God—by making his work a kind of prayer?

The book whose quotation begins Wittgenstein's own book itself begins with a quotation from a canonical text of religious praise, and quickly moves to declare that it wants itself to be (and so wants to be understood as) a work of praise from beginning to end—that is, as one long prayer.

> "You are great, Lord, and highly to be praised" (Ps. 47:2) . . .
> Man, a little piece of your creation, desires to praise you, a
> human being "bearing his mortality with him" (2 Cor. 4:10),
> carrying with him the witness of his sin and the witness that
> you "resist the proud" (1 Pet. 5:5) . . . "Grant me Lord to
> know and understand" (Ps. 118: 34, 73, 144) which comes
> first—to call upon you or to praise you, and whether know-
> ing you precedes calling upon you. But who calls upon you
> when he does not know you? For an ignorant person might
> call upon someone else instead of the right one. But surely
> you may be called upon in prayer that you may be known.
> Yet "how shall they call upon him in whom they have not
> believed? And how shall they believe without a preacher?
> (Rom. 10: 14). "They will praise the Lord who seek for him"
> (Ps. 21: 27).
> In seeking him they find him, and in finding they will
> praise him. (*Confessions*, 1.1)

Augustine declares his faith that seeking for God is a mode of praising him, and hence that a record of such a search would itself be a prayer. He thereby identifies his book as addressed before all to God, but he also identifies at least two difficulties in establishing and maintaining this prayerful relation to him. First, to want to praise God presupposes that one is worthy to give him praise, and how can an originally sinful being think of himself in such terms without succumbing to the further (or rather, without reiterating his original) sin of pride? Second, to be able to direct one's praise at its due object presupposes that one can correctly identify its addressee; but to be originally sinful is to be always already oriented away from the Truth, who is God—to lack not only the Truth but also the capacity to grasp it. How, then, can sinful human beings even begin to seek God, and thereby successfully praise him?

Both difficulties arise from the nature of the praise giver; but there are also difficulties arising from the nature of the one being praised, which Augustine devotes the first five sections of book 1 to enumerating. For if God is the omniscient and omnipresent Creator of the world, how can we call upon him, and more specifically call upon him to come to us, to be with us? That is, to what location do we address our prayer, how can the Creator come to a location within His creation, and how can he not already be wherever we are prayerfully entreating him to come? How can Augustine intelligibly intend to tell his autobiographical tale to someone who already knows everything there is to know about its subject; why does he assume that he might care about any of it? And how could any human words of praise, however heartfelt, even begin to measure up to the infinite merits of this object—how could they not fail to be worthy, as their enunciator fails to be worthy?

Augustine finds the solution to his difficulties by attaining a deeper understanding of the Creator and of this piece of his creation, and he portrays himself as doing this by engaging in a Gadamerian dialogue with scripture—more specifically, by putting into dialogue two canonical books of the Bible: the Genesis account of Creation, and the opening verses of the Gospel of St. John. For Genesis tells us that God created the world in and through speech—that creation was a divine speech act: "In the beginning God created the heaven and the earth. And the earth was without form, and void; and darkness was upon the face of the deep. And the Spirit of God moved upon the face of the waters. And God said, Let there be light: and there was light." Of the same beginning, St. John tells us: "In the beginning was the Word, and the Word was with God, and the Word was God. The same was in the beginning with God. All things were made by him; and without him was not anything that was made. In him was life; and the life was the light of men. And the light shineth in darkness; and the darkness comprehended it not."

Augustine takes John to draw out the implications of the fact that divine speech cannot be understood in terms of human speech acts—that is, as an essentially spatiotemporal phenomenon, a created event; it must rather be seen as the condition for the possibility of those (and indeed of any other of the) phenomena of creation. For speech to be the mode of divine creation, it must be an expression of the divine nature—the primordial form in which the Godhead lives and moves and has its being. In short, God does not speak; he is Speech. He does not have words; he is the Word. Since both texts associate creation with light, they imply that speech is primordially a medium of illumination, a structure of understanding or comprehension, a bulwark against chaos and darkness. And if the act of creation is effected in and through speech, what it effects and sustains must itself be thought of as a kind of utterance, an expression of the divine nature and hence an expression of the Word.

For Augustine all created beings speak of God insofar as they exist, and this speech is a form of praise:

They . . . cry aloud that they have not made themselves: "The manner of our existence shows that we are made. For before we came to be, we did not exist to be able to make ourselves." And the voice with which they speak is self-evidence. You, Lord, who are beautiful, made them for they are beautiful. You are good, for they are good. You are, for they are. Yet they are not beautiful or good or possessed of being in the sense that you their Maker are. In comparison with you they are deficient in beauty and goodness and being. (*Confessions*, 11.4)

The praise that created things offer to God by virtue of their existence is precisely calibrated to its object, because it is the nature and reality of that object that speaks through them. Their createdness is an exact measure of their Creator: it declares his reality as creator, and declares it as itself uncreated, hence both continuous and discontinuous with creation. But insofar as the nature of that creation and so of its Creator pertains to the Word, then those created beings possessed of speech are best placed to give expression to that Wordliness. They do so implicitly in any act of speaking, insofar as it aims to reveal a given aspect of reality as it truly is, explicitly by devoting their words to the business of praising God, but most aptly by finding words that praise God by showing how the whole of creation is a prayer to God: in short, by such passages of writing as the one I just quoted, and by the composition of books such as the one from which that passage comes. Such words of praise can be sure of measuring up to their object precisely because they declare, in all humility, that their ultimate source is not the one enunciating them but the One who created, sustains, and dwells within him.

For Augustine, then, in any human prayer the one addressed and the one addressing are always ultimately one and the same; hence we need have no grounds for doubting its worth, for we can understand why it is the very distance between our prayerful words and the divine reality that (by its enactment of the discontinuity between Creator and creation) shows forth God's true nature, and hence understand how the heart of an originally sinful creature can nonetheless always already be inhabited by God—can be what St. Paul pictures as a Christian epistle, written with the Spirit on the fleshy tables of the human heart. But John's Gospel further suggests that this underlying unity between the human and the divine achieved its most pure and transparent expression in the life of one human being, the one who was also divine—the Word who was made flesh and dwelt amongst his creation, and thereby brought within their reach both the Truth and a renewed capacity to grasp it.

This prefiguring of the doctrine of the Incarnation immediately introduces a Trinitarian inflection to the Genesis vision, by reconceiving the inner life of God as itself an endless dialogue between three conversation partners who are also one and the same—the divine as an enacted discourse of and about truth, beauty, and goodness, a discursive self-relation that incorporates all of reality. But it would also lead us to expect that the nature of incarnate divinity alone would itself have an intimate connection with discourse or conversation—a particular affinity for words in fruitful exchange about and with reality. And so it appears in St. Luke's Gospel, the final chapter of which (as it happens, the chapter of the New Testament immediately preceding the first chapter of St. John's Gospel) is devoted to the first appearance of the Risen Christ, and hence to his first full-fledged manifestation as Redeemer.

> And behold, two of them went that same day to a village called Emmaus, which was from Jerusalem about threescore furlongs. And they talked together of all these thing which had happened.
>
> And it came to pass that, while they communed together and reasoned, Jesus himself drew near and went with them. But their eyes were holden that they should not know him.
>
> And he said unto them, What manner of communications are these that ye have to one another, as ye walk and are sad?
>
> And the one of them, whose name of was Cleopas, answering said unto him, Art thou only a stranger in Jerusalem, and hast thou not known the things which are come to pass there in these days?
>
> And he said unto them, What things?
>
> And they said unto him, Concerning Jesus of Nazareth, which was a prophet mighty in deed and word before God and all the people: And how the chief priests and our rulers

delivered him to be condemned to death, and have crucified him. But we trusted that it had been he which should have redeemed Israel: and beside all this, today is the third day since these things were done. Yea, and certain women, also of our company made us astonished, which were early at the sepulchre; and when they found not his body, they came saying that they had also seen a vision of angels, which said that he was alive. And certain of them which were with us went to the sepulchre, and found it even so as the women had said: but him they saw not.

Then he said unto them, O fools, and slow of heart to believe all that the prophets have spoken: Ought not Christ to have suffered these things, and to enter into his glory? And beginning at Moses and all the prophets, he expounded unto them in all the scriptures the things concerning himself.

And they drew nigh unto the village, whither they went: and he made as though he would have gone further. But they constrained him, saying, Abide with us; for it is toward evening, and the day is far spent. And he went in to tarry with them.

And it came to pass, as he sat at meat with them, he took bread and blessed it, and brake and gave to them. And their eyes were opened, and they knew him; and he vanished out of their sight. And they said one to another, Did not our heart burn within us, while he talked with us by the way, and while he opened to us the scriptures? (Luke 24:13–32)

Christ first appears, not to those who seek his mute body in the tomb, but to two disciples traveling away from Jerusalem—as if driven to gain perspective upon the events it hosted—who are deep in conversation about what those events meant. He does so incognito, because they lack at that time any proper grasp of those events, and hence of the true identity of the individual who suffered them; and his pedagogy enlightens them about those events and about himself by relating his own existence and biography to the scriptures—that is, by presenting himself as their fulfillment, as the true topic of those texts, and hence as the locus at which God's Word is made real, made flesh. In this conversation, the extended scriptural dialogue of divinely inspired human speech about the divine culminates in a perfect coincidence of speaker, medium, and topic—the Word of God properly articulated by the Word of God in (words about) God's words.

But why, then, does not Christ's rereading of scripture immediately allow them to recognize that the subject matter is before their very eyes? Why does it require the breaking of bread? One might think that this deferral indicates the superiority of sacramental gesture to even divinely inspired and glossed human speech. But suppose instead this gesture indicates that the Word of God is spiritual food, that communion in the form of bread and wine is most fundamentally communication with the Word. Then, what allows the disciples to see that the human being before them is the being of whom scripture speaks is that being's willingness to give them the words they need with which to achieve that insight, and to accede to their request to abide or tarry with them so that they might absorb or ingest them in such a way as to make their hearts burn within them. In short, only those who are always already inhabited by God can acknowledge Him; only God's internalization through the Spirit makes the acknowledgment of God possible. To have the scripture opened to us is thus to participate in the internal discourse of divinity with itself—to allow one's distinctive nature as the being possessed by language to make clear its conditions of possibility by devoting its words to the business of interpreting the Word.

 But if the Word is the word of creative love, then simply to apply words to the world—to work toward making one's discourse adequate to whatever aspect of reality with which we are concerned—is to interpret and appraise God; to speak is to praise him. This, one might think, is why the Risen Christ vanishes at the moment at which the disciples' eyes are opened to his real nature: for he thereby declares that he now inhabits every word they say and every created thing about which they say it. Hence, praise has and needs no measure other than the realization of one's desire to say what one means and to mean what one says to other speakers about the topic of our conversation, whatever that might be. It means overcoming amentia, eschewing idle talk, denying the sophist, in every word we say—as philosophers, and as speakers. Does this remove the burden of praise, or absolutize it?

Notes

INTRODUCTION: *Discursive Conditions*

1. This article is collected in Rhees, *Discussions of Wittgenstein*.

2. Gaita, "Language and Conversation"; for Phillips, see particularly the opening chapter of his *Philosophy's Cool Place*; for Horn, see chap. 5 of his *Gadamer and Wittgenstein on the Unity of Language*.

ONE: *Language, Philosophy, and Sophistry*

1. My account is based on the posthumous edition of Rhees's extensive writings around this topic, entitled *Wittgenstein and the Possibility of Discourse*.

2. See secs. 12–13 of my *Inheritance and Originality*.

3. I elaborate upon this point, and develop the response to Rhees's worries about what it might permit, in secs. 17 and 18 of *Inheritance and Originality*.

4. I am thinking here of Robert Pogue Harrison's wonderful book *Forests: The Shadow of Civilization*.

5. See Murdoch, *Metaphysics as a Guide to Morals*.

6. For more on the centrality of this issue, and for a critical evaluation of the anxieties it understandably but erroneously raises in philosophers much influenced by Wittgenstein and Rhees, see my "Wittgenstein's Temple" (forthcoming).

7. See Rhees, *Wittgenstein and the Possibility of Discourse*, 39.

TWO: *Contributions to a Conversation*

1. I discuss at more length the difficult question of how far these ways of putting things simply reflect Heidegger's own thinking, and how far they

elaborate it in directions he is at least sometimes minded explicitly to reject, in chap. 5 of my *Heidegger and "Being and Time."*

2. The key Gadamerian text is *Truth and Method.* In his recent book *Gadamer and Wittgenstein on the Unity of Language,* which I cite in my introduction, Patrick Rogers Horn argues that Gadamer's attempts to characterize the fundamental relation of language to reality oscillate between brilliant insights into the ways metaphysicians distort that relation and expressions of those same metaphysical impulses, with the latter tending to predominate. Although I think that Horn misrepresents the proportion of insight to obfuscation in Gadamer (in large part because he does not take sufficiently seriously the degree to which Gadamer is simply extending insights of Heidegger, and hence is assuming Heidegger's distinctive sense of the way in which personal and philosophical modes of authenticity interweave), he makes a strong case for identifying a self-subversive tendency in some of Gadamer's thinking. Those convinced by that case might therefore wish to think of what follows as my attempt to isolate one vital strand of argument from Gadamer's antimetaphysical side, and to think of Gadamer himself as closer to Oakeshott than to Heidegger in the taxonomy of uses of the idea of a conversation that this chapter proposes—that is, as someone who deploys it ambivalently rather than authentically.

3. See, e.g., chaps. 14 and 15 of MacIntyre, *After Virtue.*

4. A more detailed critique of the purportedly Wittgensteinian bases of Rorty's misconception can be found in chap. 8 of my and Adam Swift's *Liberals and Communitarians.*

THREE: *Lectures and Letters as Conversation*

1. I have omitted Cavell's numbering of these features.

2. The essay is "The Avoidance of Love," first published in *Must We Mean What We Say?*

3. I have used the 1967 Oxford University Press edition of Schiller's letters (hereafter cited as *AEM*). Since, however, there are many editions in common use, all references to this text will be given in the form of letter number and paragraph number.

4. My citations from these letters are from the Cooper edition of Plato cited in the bibliography.

5. I discuss Cavell's notion of "myth" in the introduction to *Inheritance and Originality* (18–21).

6. Translated by J. Glenn Gray as *What Is Called Thinking?* The following six paragraphs are indebted to portions of my "Reading, Writing, Re-membering."

1. This is a pervasive theme in Cavell's most recent collection of essays, *Philosophy the Day after Tomorrow*, to which this conclusion is in a sense a response.

2. The force and ambivalence of these Platonic anxieties are well brought out in chap. 3 of Andrea Wilson Nightingale's *Genres in Dialogue*.

3. From a 1949 letter to M. O'C. Drury; see R. Rhees, ed., *Recollections of Wittgenstein*, x–xvi.

Bibliography

Augustine. *Confessions.* Trans. H. Chadwick. Oxford: Oxford University Press, 1991.

Cavell, S. *Cities of Words: Pedagogical Letters on a Register of the Moral Life.* Cambridge Mass.: Harvard University Press, 2004.

———. *The Claim of Reason: Wittgenstein, Skepticism, Morality, and Tragedy.* Oxford: Oxford University Press, 1979.

———. *Conditions Handsome and Unhandsome: The Constitution of Emersonian Perfectionism.* Chicago: University of Chicago Press, 1990.

———. *Must We Mean What We Say? A Book of Essays.* Cambridge: Cambridge University Press, 1969.

———. *Philosophy the Day after Tomorrow.* Cambridge, Mass.: Harvard University Press, 2005.

———. *Pursuits of Happiness: The Hollywood Comedy of Remarriage.* Cambridge, Mass.: Harvard University Press, 1981.

———. *Themes Out of School: Effects and Causes.* San Francisco: North Point Press, 1984.

Gadamer, H.-G. *Truth and Method.* London: Sheed and Ward, 1975.

Gaita, R. "Language and Conversation: Wittgenstein's Builders." In *Wittgenstein: Centenary Essays,* ed. A. Phillips Griffiths. Cambridge: Cambridge University Press, 1991.

Harrison, R. Pogue. *Forests: The Shadow of Civilization.* Chicago: University of Chicago Press, 1992.

Heidegger, M. *Being and Time.* Trans. J. Macquarrie and E. Robinson. Oxford: Blackwell, 1962.

———. *What Is Called Thinking?* Trans. J. Glenn Gray. New York: Harper and Row, 1968.

Horn, P. Rogers. *Gadamer and Wittgenstein on the Unity of Language.* London: Ashgate, 2005.

MacIntyre, A. *After Virtue.* London: Duckworth, 1981.

Mulhall, S. *Heidegger and "Being and Time."* 2nd ed. London: Routledge, 2005.

———. *Inheritance and Originality: Wittgenstein, Heidegger, Kierkegaard.* Oxford: Oxford University Press, 2001.

———. "Reading, Writing, Re-membering: What Heidegger and Cavell Call Thinking." In *Ordinary Language Criticism,* ed. K. Dauber and W. Jost. Evanston: Northwestern University Press, 2003.

———. "Wittgenstein's Temple: Three Styles of Philosophical Architecture." Forthcoming.

Mulhall, S., and A. Swift. *Liberals and Communitarians.* 2nd ed. Oxford: Blackwell, 1996.

Murdoch, I. *Metaphysics as a Guide to Morals.* London: Chatto and Windus, 1992.

Nightingale, A. Wilson. *Genres in Dialogue: Plato and the Construct of Philosophy.* Cambridge: Cambridge University Press, 1995.

Oakeshott, M. *Rationalism in Politics.* Indianapolis: Liberty Fund, 1962.

Phillips, D. Z. *Philosophy's Cool Place.* Ithaca, N.Y.: Cornell University Press, 1999.

Plato. *Complete Works.* Ed. J. Cooper. Indianapolis: Hackett, 1997.

Rhees, R. *Discussions of Wittgenstein.* London: Routledge and Kegan Paul, 1970.

———, ed. *Recollections of Wittgenstein.* Oxford: Oxford University Press, 1984.

———. *Wittgenstein and the Possibility of Discourse.* Ed. D. Z. Phillips. Cambridge: Cambridge University Press, 1998.

Rorty, R. *Philosophy and the Mirror of Nature.* Princeton: Princeton University Press, 1979.

Schiller, F. *On the Aesthetic Education of Man.* Trans. E. Wilkinson and L. Willoughby. Oxford: Oxford University Press, 1967.

Wittgenstein, L. *Philosophical Investigations.* Trans. G. E. M. Anscombe. Oxford: Blackwell, 1953.

Index

Adam, 13–14, 43
adolescence, 77–78
Aesthetic Education of Man, The
  (Schiller), 80–85
Alceste, 77–78, 89
ambiguity, 53–54
amentia, 54–55, 83, 102, 110
appearance vs. reality, 36, 53
Aristotle, 43, 58, 93
art, 9, 73, 84–85, 100–101
Augustine, 14–15, 103–6
authenticity, 50–52, 55, 57, 84

Bach, Johann Sebastian, 102–3
Being, 8–11, 41–47
Being and Time (Heidegger), 8, 41–
  58, 97, 101
Being-oneself, 50–52, 57–58
Being-with, 50–52, 57–58
builders, 16–22, 28

Cavell, Stanley, 3, 8–10, 33–34,
  54–55, 67–98, 99–100, 101, 111,
  112, 113
Cities of Words (Cavell), 3, 9, 67–98,
  99–100

Claim of Reason, The (Cavell),
  54–55, 77, 101–2
comedies of remarriage, 68
Confessions (Augustine), 14–15,
  103–6
conformity, 83
conscience, 55–56
creation, 14, 43, 104–6
curiosity, 53–54

Dasein, 47–58
demand, 55
democracy, 75, 78
desire, 82–85, 99, 110
dialogue, 30, 32, 37–38, 49, 56,
  60–61, 91, 107
discourse, 32–36, 38, 48, 55, 109
discursive unity, 3, 28–30

edification, 64, 85
education, 71–76
Emerson, Ralph Waldo, 66, 72–
  77, 74, 79, 81–82, 84, 86
emotivism, 35
Enlightenment, the, 60
essence, 19–21, 26, 101
evil, 37

family resemblance, 26–27
finitude, 59
form of life, 47
friendship, 58, 93
fundamental ontology, 44–45, 50

Gadamer, Hans-Georg, 58–61, 98, 104
Gadamer and Wittgenstein on the Unity of Language (Horn), 4, 111, 112
Gaita, Rai, 4, 7, 11
Genesis, 13–14, 43, 104–5
Genres in Dialogue (Nightingale), 113
Gospel of St. John, 104–7
Gospel of St. Luke, 107–10
grammar, 101–2

Harrison, Robert Pogue, 111
Heidegger, Martin, 1, 7–8, 9–10, 41–58, 94–97, 99, 101
hermeneutics, 44, 58–61
history, 58–61
Holland, Roy, 7
Horn, Patrick Rogers, 4, 111, 112

Ibsen, Henrik, 86–87
idle talk, 52–55, 57, 110
individuality, 21–23, 52, 55, 57, 84, 110

justice, 34–35, 74–75

Kant, Immanuel, 46–47, 81
King Lear (Shakespeare), 79

language, 26–28, 109
language-games, 23–27, 36
lecture, form of, 3, 68–75

letters, 76–98
Liberals and Communitarians (Swift), 112

MacIntyre, Alasdair, 61, 112
Man, das, 50–52, 57–58
melodramas of the unknown woman, 68, 77
Mill, John Stuart, 82–83
Molière, 76–78
moral perfectionism, 9, 56–58, 67–98, 99–100
Murdoch, Iris, 31, 111
myth, 92

naming, 14–16
Nietzsche, Friedrich, 7, 31, 66, 70, 73, 96
Nightingale, Andrea Wilson, 113
nihilism, 66

Oakeshott, Michael, 61–63
ontic vs ontological, 44
orders, 17–18
original sin, 59, 88–89, 104, 106
Othello (Shakespeare), 78–79

Parfit, Derek, 31
Paul, St., 85–89, 98, 106
passionate speech, 93–94
phenomenological method, 47–48
Phillips, D. Z., 4, 5, 7, 11
philosophy, 30–39, 44–48, 65–66, 73–74, 80–81, 92–93, 99–101, 110
Plato, 1, 34–39, 48–49, 70, 89–94, 100
play, 24, 84–85
praise, 99–110
prayer, 103–6

Rawls, John, 73–74
reality, 14, 21–23, 30, 34–39, 46–47, 49, 61, 62, 64–65, 106
receptivity, 14, 59
regional ontology, 44–45
religion, 10–11, 85–89, 99–110
Republic, The (Plato), 34–36, 70
Rhees, Rush, 4–7, 9, 10, 16–39, 40, 45–47, 50, 56, 61, 111
Rorty, Richard, 63–66, 112

Schiller, Friedrich, 80–85, 97, 112
self, 55–57, 70, 96
self-reliance, 74
Seventh Letter, The (Plato), 89–94
skepticism, 34, 35–36
Socrates, 34–36, 100
sophistry, 6, 8, 34–39, 48–50, 63–66, 110
speaking, 17–18, 20–23, 25–26, 34–35, 95, 102, 105–6, 109–10

textual meaning, 59
they-self, 50–52, 57–58

Thoreau, Henry David, 79
Thrasymachus, 34–36, 39
Tractatus Logico-Philosophicus (Wittgenstein), 27
Trinity, 106–7

uncanny, 12, 56
understanding, growth of, 21–22, 30, 32, 53, 61, 65, 68
United States of America, 78–79
unity of culture, 28–30
unity of language, 26–30

virtues, 23

What Is Called Thinking? (Heidegger), 94–97, 99
Wittgenstein, Ludwig, 15–17, 23–27, 40, 101–3
Wittgenstein and the Possibility of Discourse (Rhees), 4, 16–39
words, 20–21, 105
writing, 90–91, 95

Page-Barbour and Richard Lectures
(IN PRINT)

SIR JOHN SUMMERSON
The Architecture of Victorian London

JOHANNES FABIAN
Moments of Freedom: Anthropology and Popular Culture

IAN HACKING
Mad Travelers: Reflections on the Reality of Transient Mental Illnesses

HARVIE FERGUSON
Modernity and Subjectivity: Body, Soul, Spirit

STEPHEN MULHALL
The Conversation of Humanity